The Heart of Silence

**Contemplative Prayer
by Those
Who Practise It**

Praise for
The Heart of Silence

"In his *Evangeli Nuntiandi,* Paul VI stressed that today's youth will only follow masters whose lives exemplify their teaching. This new selection of fascinating accounts painstakingly collected by Paul Harris is the proof that the faithful – priests, religious and laity – have a burning desire for contemplative prayer. It also shows that Christian Meditation as taught by John Main is the form of silent prayer preferred by a large number of people from various countries. This is what the Church has been waiting for to fulfil the hopes of Vatican II."

Cardinal Jean Margéot
Mauritius

"This treasure of a book represents 'a cloud of witnesses' to the efficacy of the practice of contemplative prayer, with each contributor revealing how the Spirit brings forth her gifts from within every size and shape of seeker.

Frank X. Tuoti
Author of Why Not Be a Mystic?
Tucson, Arizona

"Paul Harris sets a loving and beautiful table and then invites us to come to the feast he has so artfully prepared. At this feast we are engaged at a profound level as people from all walks of life share significant aspects of their spiritual search, their struggles, their perseverance (and lack of it), their commitment to the discovery of Truth and Love. This collection of short spiritual biographies feeds and inspires the hunger of spiritual seekers."

Sr. Eileen O'Hea
Psychotherapist, author and spiritual director
Roseville, Minnesota

The Heart of Silence

Contemplative Prayer
by Those
Who Practise It

Edited by Paul T. Harris

Other books by Paul T. Harris

Brief to the Bishops: Canadian Catholic Lay People Speak Their Minds. Longman's Canada Ltd., 1965.
Genealogical History of the Harris Family of Worcester, England. Privately printed, 1971.
John Main by Those Who Knew Him. Novalis and Darton, Longman and Todd, 1991.
The Fire of Silence and Stillness: An Anthology of Quotations for the Spiritual Journey. Templegate and Darton, Longman and Todd, 1995.
Christian Meditation: Contemplative Prayer for a New Generation. Novalis and Darton, Longman and Todd, 1996.
Silence and Stillness in Every Season: Daily Readings with John Main. Continuum and Darton, Longman and Todd, 1997.

© Novalis, Saint Paul University, Ottawa, 1999.

Cover design: Blair Turner

Layout: Gilles Lépine

Novalis, 49 Front St. East, Second Floor
  Toronto, Ontario M5E 1B3
  1-800-387-7164 or (416) 363-3303

First published in 1999 by Novalis, Saint Paul University, Ottawa, Canada
  and Darton, Longman and Todd Ltd, 1 Spencer Court,
  140-142 Wandsworth High Street, London SW18 4JJ U.K.

All rights reserved. No part of this publication may be reproduced, stored in a retrieval system, or transmitted in any form, or by any means, electronic, mechanical, photocopying, recording or otherwise, without the written permission of the publisher.

We acknowledge the financial support of the Government of Canada through the Book Publishing Development Program for our publishing activities.

Canadian Cataloguing in Publication Data

Main entry under title:

The heart of silence: contemplative prayer by those who practise it

ISBN 2-89507-021-0

1. Meditation – Christianity. I. Harris, Paul T. (Paul Turner), 1926-

BV4813.H42 1999   248.3'4   C99-900963-X

A catalogue record for this book is available from the British Library

ISBN 0-232-52361-4

Printed in Canada

Contents and Contributors

Introduction.................................... 11

Chapter 1
    The Call to Meditation:
    "The Second Knock on the Door"............... 17
        Elizabeth Byrnes
        Len Connor
        Denise McMahon

Chapter 2
    The Difficulties of Getting Started:
    "The Mantra: A Reed Against a Hurricane"...... 31
        Nina Carpenter
        Joe Doerfer
        Ed Falchiere
        Julie F. Felton
        Sheila Geary
        Suzy T. Kane

Chapter 3
    On Trying Different Traditions of Meditation:
    "The Search Is On"........................... 51
        Joseph L. Barcello

Dorothy Deakin
Lionel E. Goulet
Pat Kasmarik
James Logan
William Mishler
Isobel Page
Jo Russell
Frank Seeburger

Chapter 4
On Discovering John Main:
"The Teacher I Had Been Looking For" 79
Steve Cartwright
John Cotling
Yvonne (Main) Fitzgerald
Gregory J. Ryan
— Madeleine Simon 92
Sheila Walshe

Chapter 5
Meditation and Married Life:
"It Has Deepened Our Relationship" 99
Robbie Bishop
Tom Cain
Maurie Costello
Patricia Gulick
Leon Milroy
Marlene Sweeney
Judi Taylor

Chapter 6
Meditation and the Priesthood:
"We Are All Beginners" 123
Frank Cassidy
Peter A. De Marco
Frank Delia
John Jay Hughes
Denis Mahony

— Michael Mifsud 141
— Henri Tardy 145
— Seraphim Thomas 148
— David Wood

Chapter 7
Meditation, Aging, Illness and Death: "Hitting Rock Bottom" 155
— Joyce Donoghue
Al of Hobart
Nancy Kadrovach
David A. Kruse
—Mary Orth-Pallavicini
—Carol McDonough
Bonye Norton
Antoinette O'Reilly
Katharine Thomas
Donna Wojtyna
Sheila Wood
—Serena Woon

Chapter 8
The Fruits of Meditation: "A Change Has Taken Place in Me" 193
Peter Collins
Karen Deley
Hilda Frost
Irene Koroi
Bob Lukey
Mary Lou McCluskey
Evelyn McDevitt
Carol Peterson

Contributors Grouped by Countries. 217

The World Community for Christian Meditation 221

Acknowledgements

This book is dedicated to its 60 contributors, who so generously testify to a deep understanding of the path of silence and stillness in contemplative prayer. They speak from their hearts about the practice of Christian Meditation and convince us by spiritual power and not with specious arguments, a reminder of the powerful words of St. Paul:

The word I spoke to you, the gospel I proclaimed did not sway you with subtle arguments; it carried conviction by spiritual power, so that your faith might be built, not upon human wisdom but upon the power of God. (1 Corinthians 2:4-5)

I am also indebted to the British publisher Darton, Longman and Todd for permission to quote excerpts from the books *John Main by Those Who Knew Him; The Fire of Silence and Stillness: An Anthology of Quotations for the Spiritual Journey;* and *The Way of Unknowing*. I also acknowledge Bloodaxe Books for a poem by R.S. Thomas in the contribution by David Wood.

My particular thanks go to Sr. Marian McCarthy of Roselle, Illinois, who in the past few years has so ably edited the American Christian Meditation newsletter. I am thankful to Marian for permission to reprint a number of testimonials found in the newsletter.

Sincere thanks again to Carol Nixon, who has used her word processing skill in yet another one of my books. And a final thanks to all those whose contributions were not published because of lack of space. Their spirit and enthusiasm helped me greatly as I wove many people's personal stories into this book.

Paul T. Harris

Introduction

One of the most important spiritual movements of our time has been the contemporary worldwide renewal in the practice of contemplative prayer or, as it is more commonly called these days, Christian Meditation.

But what is the *experience* of those who have entered the daily silence and stillness of this way of prayer? This book attempts to answer that question as 60 men and women from various countries around the world speak openly and freely about their own personal pilgrimage of meditation and how it has affected their lives. My hope is that these inspiring stories will lead many others to undertake this pilgrimage.

In the stories that appear in this book we can see at a glance that no age, level, gender, culture or religious tradition has a monopoly on spiritual wisdom. The stories show us that the inner call and contemplative experience are the same everywhere: a longing for the absolute in the silence of one's heart. The men and women who speak in this book have a common mission to relate their particular time, age and circumstances to eternity and the things of the Spirit.

The contributors to this book are indeed *teachers* in every sense of that word, as they provide instruction, encouragement, insights, practical wisdom, charm, amusement and often surprising paradoxes. They also highlight key teachings of the Benedictine monk John Main (1926–1982) on the practice of Christian Meditation.

But newcomers about to read this book might first ask: *What is the practice of Christian Meditation all about? Why should one meditate? How does one meditate?* And who is John Main? First, to John Main.

John Main: His Life and Teaching

John Main lived only 56 years (1926–1982), but in that time became a journalist, soldier, law student, diplomat, university lecturer, Benedictine monk and finally one of the great contemporary teachers of contemplative prayer and one of the twentieth century's most important spiritual guides.

His journeys took him from London, England, to Ireland, Rome, Malaysia, Washington, D.C., and finally to Montreal, Canada, where he founded a Benedictine monastery dedicated to teaching this way of prayer. But John Main's greatest journey was *inwards,* towards the centre. He understood fully these words of Jesus:

> *The kingdom of God does not come in such a way as to be seen. No one will say "Look, here it is" or "There it is," because the kingdom of God is within you.* (Luke 17:20-21)

This became John Main's final journey: leading thousands of people around the world to the discovery of this "kingdom within" through the daily, disciplined practice of Christian Meditation. His teaching, based on scripture and the prayer practice of the early-fourth-century desert monks, has now spread to 60 countries.

John Main tells us that to be with God we do not require words, thoughts or images, but the silent consciousness of *a Presence.* He reminds us that our spiritual pilgrimage has no future unless we have the courage to become more and more silent. In fact, our journey will not even start unless we are willing to accept the discipline of the daily practice of silence and inner stillness.

John Main also saw the need for meditators to meet together each week; since his death over 1,300 meditation groups have sprung up around the world.

Why Meditate?

St. Augustine once said, "We must first be restored to ourselves that, making in ourselves as it were a stepping-stone, we may rise thence and be borne up to God." John Main reminds us that meditation is not primarily a way of "doing" but a way of "becoming": becoming ourselves and coming to self-knowledge. He says that in this way of prayer we seek to become the person we are called to be.

Meister Eckhart (1260–1327), the great medieval spiritual teacher, also recognized that the question of God is a question about self-knowledge. He said that we cannot know God unless we first know ourselves, and we can only know ourselves by a return to the human heart. Says Eckhart,

> The sublime and glorious reality which we call God, is to be sought first and foremost in the human heart. If we do not find him there, we shall not find him anywhere else. If we do find him there, we can never lose him again; wherever we turn, we shall see his face.

To Find God in the Human Heart

That is why we meditate: we seek God's presence within our own heart. The unforgettable words of St. Augustine in his *Confessions* confirm this truth:

> O beauty ever ancient, ever new.
> Too late have I loved you.
> I was outside, and you were within me.

And I never found you until I found you
within myself.

John Main says that meditation is a way to enter the living stream of love within our own hearts, and that the silence each of us is summoned to enter is the eternal silence of God. This silence, says John Main, each one of us can find within ourselves.

The essence of meditation, then, is our desire for God: we are waiting on God, we are listening to God, we are resting in God. St. Augustine put it succinctly:

You have made us for yourself O Lord, and our hearts are restless until they rest in thee.

Meditation is nothing less than the transformation of our hearts. As one fourth-century desert father said:

Unless there is a still centre in the middle of the storm,
Unless a person in the midst of all their activities preserves a secret room in their heart where they stand in silence before God,
Then they will lose all sense of spiritual direction and be torn to pieces.

When we meditate we go into that secret place, that still centre. And out of that stillness, as we turn towards God, comes the life of the Spirit by which we are transformed into love. We meditate to open ourselves to the birth of Christ within.

The interesting thing is that the fruits of prayer enter our life almost immediately so that, if we persevere on the path of meditation, the love of God overflows in our life. This love will overflow in our lives in a thousand ways. In Chapter 8, the contributors to this book talk about the connection between prayer and action. But John Main warns us that we can become intoxicated by words when the only important thing is to enter daily into the experience itself in faithfulness and commitment. The experience itself, says John Main, will teach us the "why" of meditation.

John Main further points out that if we are faithful and patient, meditation will bring us into deeper and deeper realms of silence. It is in this silence that we are led into the mystery of the eternal silence of God. That is the invitation of Christian prayer, says John Main: *"to lose ourselves and to be absorbed in God."*

How to Meditate

The thing that surprises most newcomers to Christian Meditation is its *simplicity*. John Main always emphasizes how simple it is to enter into the experience of meditation. In his book *The Way of Unknowing* he says:

> *Sit down. Sit still and upright. Close your eyes lightly. Sit relaxed but alert. Silently, interiorly begin to say a single word. Recite the prayer-word* Maranatha. *Recite it as four syllables of equal length,* Ma-ra-na-tha. *Listen to it as you say it, gently but continuously. Do not think or imagine anything, spiritual or otherwise. If thoughts and images come, these are distractions at the time of meditation, so keep returning to simply saying the word. Meditate each morning and evening for between twenty and thirty minutes.*

Maranatha means "Come, Lord Jesus" in Aramaic, the language Jesus spoke. It is probably the most ancient Christian prayer. St. Paul ends the first letter to the Corinthians, and St. John ends the Book of Revelation, with this word.

John Main points out that as we grow in fidelity to our prayer word, or as it is commonly called, a *mantra*, the word will grow more and more deeply rooted in us. We usually begin reciting the mantra in our head. But as we make progress the mantra becomes more familiar, less of a stranger, less of an intruder in our consciousness. We find that less effort is required to persevere in saying it throughout the time of our meditation. Then it seems that we are not so much saying it in our minds as sounding it in our hearts. This is the stage that John Main describes as the rooting of the mantra in our hearts.

Christian meditation is a daily spiritual discipline that requires patience, fidelity and commitment. It also requires simplicity, but we are led to that simplicity and childlikeness by our mantra.

Meditation is the missing contemplative dimension of Christian life today. However, it does not exclude other types of prayer and indeed deepens one's need for the sacramental life and one's reading of scripture.

The Role of the Weekly Meditation Group

Many of the contributors to this book talk about the important role of the weekly meditation group meeting. The weekly meeting provides the support and encouragement we need to carry on the daily journey with faithfulness and commitment. It is in effect a *support* group. Groups meet in diverse locations and at various hours throughout the day and evening in homes, apartments, schools, churches, rectories, religious communities, chapels, universities, prisons, office buildings, a department store, senior citizens' homes and factories.

The weekly one-hour meeting generally consists of listening to a recorded talk by John Main, followed by 25 minutes of silent meditation and a time for shared reflections or questions from newcomers. The group setting enables beginners to learn "how" to meditate while at the same time provides support and encouragement to those already "on the path."

There is a saying that one cannot sit on the riverbank of prayer. One must jump in and get wet. It is time now to listen to the contributors to this book who unwittingly play the role of modern-day prophets as we enter the twenty-first century. They tell us of a worldwide spiritual renewal in prayer taking place at this moment in history. This contemplative renewal, perhaps the best-kept secret in the Church, is gaining momentum as more and more Christians hear the call to silence and stillness in prayer and to what Thomas Merton calls "a country beyond words and beyond names."

Paul T. Harris

Chapter 1

The Call to Meditation

"The Second Knock on the Door"

Elizabeth Byrnes
Len Connor
Denise McMahon

Elizabeth Byrnes

Elizabeth Byrnes, who lives in Merville by the Bridge, County Galway, Ireland, is 46, a Catholic, and a practising solicitor. She has been married to Martin Byrnes since 1977. She received her secondary education at the Dominican Convent School and Third Level at University College, Galway and the Law Society School in Dublin. Elizabeth is a Minister of the Eucharist in her local parish, leads a Lectio Divina *weekly group and is a leader of a Christian Meditation group at the Dominican Convent, Taylor's Hill, Galway.*

My first introduction to Christian Meditation was about mid-1992. While I have always been a committed, practising Catholic, my prayer life at that time was not very satisfactory. Indeed, prayer was a somewhat intermittent activity, reaching high points in times of difficulty or trouble and receding to almost nil in between. Following my recovery from a recurrence of a very serious illness in 1989 and having gone through the trauma of my mother's death in 1990, I had, however, begun to take prayer more seriously and had started to read the scriptures on a regular basis. I had also become a daily Mass-goer and was becoming far more spiritual in my outlook on life.

However, I still found it difficult to pray, and "saying prayers" didn't give me any satisfaction at all. I felt there had to be *more* to prayer than this but I didn't know where to look for help. I found great joy and consolation and inspiration in reading the Bible and in being "with Jesus" in the scriptures, but I was searching all the time for something more. I began to pray, too, for a deeper way of prayer.

During Holy Week 1992 I took part in a week of guided prayer during which my director, who has since become a trusted friend, opened up for me new and deeper ways of praying with scripture. Scripture is still very important in my prayer life, yet I felt at the time that there was still more to prayer and that I hadn't yet found the right way for me.

A Small Book: The Gethsemani Talks

One day, probably about a month or two later, I was browsing through the library of our local diocesan centre searching for something spiritual to read, when I came across a small book entitled *Christian Meditation: The Gethsemani Talks* by Dom John Main. Not having any idea what it was about except that it looked interesting and it was a small book and probably easy to read in a day or two, I took it out on loan. Fr. John's talks, the story of his own introduction to meditation and his description of this way of prayer all struck a chord with me. I became very excited and immediately decided "that's the way for me." So I started to meditate following the instruction in the book. However, I found that it was not as easy as it sounded, and I'm afraid it wasn't long before I gave it up. But the seed was sown and, though I reverted to praying in other ways, I knew there was something missing, for I felt a sort of emptiness and longing within.

Later the same year (1992) I was in the cathedral in Galway and happened to see a notice on the door of the bookshop there. The notice gave details of a weekend of prayer and meditation taking place at Esker Monastery, a Redemptorist retreat house about nine miles from my home. The word "meditation" jumped out at me and I was immediately interested. I was also intrigued when I read that the principal speaker was a relative of mine, a Benedictine monk from Glenstal Abbey, and so I booked a place straightaway.

The Second Knock on the Door

The weekend turned out to be the annual John Main School of Prayer in Ireland, and so I had my second introduction to Christian Meditation in the space of a few months: a second knock on the door. This time, however, through listening to the talks, speaking with other meditators and, most of all, through participating in the group meditation sessions, I was totally convinced that, indeed, this *was* the way of prayer for me. This was a sort of home-coming experience, and I knew that in leading me inexorably to meditation God had answered my prayer.

It was not that it all suddenly became easy overnight, but I found myself making a commitment that weekend to follow the path of meditation to the best of my ability. This is a commitment I have never, thank God, regretted. I was also invited that weekend to join a meditation group at the Dominican convent near my old home in Taylor's Hill in Galway. I did so and am still a member. I find the weekly meetings an invaluable support on the journey. It is so good to have friends with whom to discuss problems and to share views with fellow travellers along the way.

Meditation: It's Simple, But Not Always Easy

Meditation is, to use Fr. John's words, "simple, but not easy." At times I still find it very difficult to get through the 25 minutes twice a day. More often than not I am dogged with distractions the entire time of the meditation and feel no consolation at all. But over the years I have come to realize the deep truth in the words of my first teacher of meditation, who said to me, "The distractions are the best part." In other words, in persevering despite the distractions, one gradually learns to leave *self* behind and to put one's trust in God. You find that, mysteriously, in the *nothingness* of meditation there is *everything* and that meditation is worth the perseverance despite distractions, dryness and emptiness. In meditating we learn to accept ourselves as we really are and we find that we are loved: broken, but loved. To know this in an experiential way has been a profoundly liberating event in my life.

Meditation is the deeper way of prayer for which I had been searching and praying. I simply cannot go through a day now without meditating. At the beginning I kept wondering how long it would be before I would experience all sorts of joys and insights, but I have learned, as most people do who have been meditating for some time, not to seek anything from meditation. Now I meditate because it is important for me to do so. To be "on the way" is the important thing; the rest is in God's hands.

"Lead Kindly Light, Lead Me On"

St. John of the Cross once wrote that one is ready for contemplative prayer when one is unable any longer to engage in discursive prayer using concepts and images. That is exactly the way I felt before I found meditation. Or, perhaps more correctly, before it found *me*. Words were a definite distraction; I needed to be silent, but I had never, until then, found a way of becoming silent. I used to sit as quietly as I could before an icon or a lighted candle, or by the river at the bottom of the garden, or stand under the night sky gazing at the moon and stars and try to still my mind. Indeed, I remember standing like this one night contemplating the glory of God in the myriad stars and wondering where my life was heading. The following words came into my mind as I stood there:

> "I am at a threshold.
> I stand under the stars and ask 'Where to?'
> I feel Your call in my heart, but am slow to answer.
> I gaze at Your light and say 'Lead me.'
> Where to, I do not know,
> But the call is strong, and so (like Newman) I say
> 'Lead kindly Light, lead me on.'"

For me, these words epitomize meditation and my journey to it.

The Prayer of Jesus Deep in Our Hearts

Christian Meditation is the mainstay of my prayer life but, like most meditators, I haven't dropped other forms of prayer. Like most people I pray differently at different times. But since starting to meditate, I have found that all other forms of prayer – scripture, Divine Office, the eucharist – are richer and are more meaningful. I believe that this is because in meditation, and in trying to let go of everything, we allow ourselves and all our prayer and all our activities to be gathered up and swept along by the prayer of Jesus sounding deep in our hearts.

I feel very fortunate and privileged to have been led to meditation and I will always be deeply grateful to God for it. I am deeply thankful to God, too, for sending me a teacher in the early days after I first started to meditate. The fact that I am so totally committed to the way is, I believe, owing in no small measure to the promise I made to my friend and teacher that I would not give up before I had given it at least six months. By that time, he said, I would know if it was *the* way of prayer for me, and he was right.

Len Connor

Len Connor was born in 1925 and worked 10 years as an architect in Australia and 35 years in the UK. He served with the Royal Engineers (1942–47) and was commissioned and posted to India (1943–1946). A cradle Catholic and married, he has been active in the Rite of Christian Initiation of Adults, leads a Christian Meditation group at his home and volunteers his service one day a week at the World Community for Christian Meditation International Centre in London, England.

Somebody once said that it is remarkable how many "coincidences" are experienced in connection with prayer, particularly intercessory prayer. The story of my coming to the practice of Christian Meditation is a series of such coincidences.

It began in the spring of 1992. I seemed then to be in the doldrums of my spiritual life. I felt that I needed to grow or develop spiritually in some way and I felt stuck in a rut. I felt that my attendance at Mass was a routine and was the result of the mere habit of a lifetime rather than an actively chosen participation. Prayer seemed empty. I decided to pray to be taught *how* to pray.

On the "Mumbo-Jumbo" of the Mantra

Shortly afterwards, I was near Westminster Cathedral bookshop and thought I would do some browsing. I had no particular object or interest in mind. After picking up one or two books I happened to glance at John Main's *The Inner Christ*. On riffling through it I saw mention of the mantra and my highly prejudiced reaction was to have nothing to do with what I thought was some kind of mumbo-jumbo. I hastily put the book back on the shelf and left the bookshop.

By coincidence I had an appointment that same day to visit my former parish priest, who was living in retirement on the eastern outskirts of London, a good two-hour train journey from my home. I had by some strange urge been moved to look up his name and telephone number in the Catholic Directory. As I had not seen him or been in touch with him for 30 years, that desire to contact him seemed a bit odd. What point was there to it?

I arrived and found the old priest to be bowed with age, but still with a bright and perceptive mind. We chatted about old times and finally got on to a discussion about the practice of mental or discursive prayer. He told me that this was a way of deeper prayer than the prayer of petition but that I would be tempted to regard it as boring and a waste of time. He added, however, that a woman was coming by shortly who would be able to tell me more about it.

Seeking God in Silence and Stillness

The good woman duly arrived, and after introductions my priest friend explained what we had been talking about and asked her to enlarge on mental prayer for me. The first thing she did was to correct him: mental prayer was different from the prayer she practised. She was meditating using a mantra and seeking God in silence and stillness in daily periods of contemplative prayer. She talked about Christian Meditation and convinced me that I indeed should have bought John Main's book at the bookshop after all.

Not One, Not Two, But Three "Coincidences"

So far, three "coincidences." *One*, noticing John Main's book out of many others in the bookshop; *two*, for some reason making a date to meet a priest I hadn't seen in many years; *three*, my visit happening at the very time a meditator was calling on my old friend. There was more to come. My priest friend had come to the point of needing full-time care, and he moved to a home to spend his last days. The meditator I had met invited me to go with her and another woman to visit him one day. When we were there she suggested a period of meditation, and so I experienced my first group meditation.

This woman had also given me the address of the London Christian Meditation Centre, where I soon went for a midday meditation. In the meantime I purchased *The Inner Christ*. I also found out from the Centre that a weekend retreat was to be held at London's Damascus House. The retreat leader was Fr. Laurence Freeman, a confrere of Fr. John Main, of whom I had no knowledge at that time.

A Teacher I Would Want to Hear Again

I arrived early at Damascus House and went into the dining room for a cup of tea. There were only one or two people there. One youngish man in casual dress who was wearing a cross on a cord round his neck got up and came over to say hello. He said how nice it was to see me again. I didn't want to embarrass him by saying we had never met so we went on to exchange a few pleasantries. Later on I was surprised to see him in a monk's habit and to realize that he was Dom Laurence, the giver of the retreat. The theme was "Aspects of Love." I quickly realized that I had met a teacher whom I should want to hear again and again. I was hooked on Christian Meditation. I bought some audiotapes and when I returned home invited a group of friends, including our parish priest, to come and listen to them. This proved to be the beginning of my own meditation group.

My wife received the revelation that I had become a meditator with some barely concealed doubts. I should like to be able to end with the good news that she joins me in this path of prayer. The answer to that is, *not yet*, which implies that it may happen one day. Meanwhile my daily meditation is for both of us, because after many years of marriage we share most things.

If This Isn't the Work of the Spirit...

So my route to the practice of Christian Meditation has been a bit circuitous: prayer of petition made without even dreaming of the sort of answer I might receive, a bookshop, a curious urge to look up an old parish priest, a meditator who happened to come that day to our meeting, a first group experience, a call at the London Meditation Centre, a decision to book a retreat led by Fr. Laurence. And here I am, yours truly, a Christian meditator. If this isn't the work of the Spirit, I don't know what is.

Sr. Denise McMahon sm

Sr. Denise McMahon from Australia is a member of the Missionary Sisters of the Society of Mary. After professional studies she was missioned to Bougainville where she taught in a girls' secondary school for six years. She then went to a francophone Catholic secondary school in Vanuatu for four years and for the past six years has been a lecturer at Corpus Christi Teachers College, Fiji. She has also been given permission by her congregation to be a member of the Marist Contemplative Community outside Suva, Fiji, which seeks to create a space where people are welcome to enter for prayer, reflection and stillness.

I am writing this while on holiday in a Fijian village situated on an island renowned for its sparkling, crystal-clear coral sea, pristine white sand and unspoiled rainforests dotted with magical waterfalls and cool, refreshing streams. The people, too, are renowned for their friendliness, warmth and hospitality. One lady, Tema, reserves the main room of her small thatched house for prayer and, morning and evening, I meditate there with Mere from the Marist Contemplative Community, who has invited me to her village for the holidays.

When we first came we explained to Tema how to meditate. She joined us, along with her elderly father-in-law who would come out of his room when we arrived and sit with us. He died last night, unexpectedly and peacefully and with his family around him. As I write, the villagers are busy preparing for his funeral to be held in a couple of hours' time. I feel close to the old man because of the times shared with him in silent prayer.

I was introduced to Christian Meditation about 10 years ago at home on holiday when one of my sisters gave me two of her tapes of talks by John Main. I listened to them, put them in a drawer and forgot about them until I was reminded each time I returned home and opened that particular drawer. Finally, on leave at home last year, I took the tapes out, listened to them and, finding they were still clear, put them in my suitcase and brought them back to Fiji. They are now part of the small library on meditation at the Nazareth Prayer Centre.

Getting Hit on the Head Twice

They say some people are hit twice before they come to Christian Meditation; that was probably my first hit. The second hit was four years ago when Fr. Denis Mahony, whom I first knew when I had been sent for cross-cultural experience to his mission station in the heart of Bougainville 26 years ago, gently invited me to a series of Saturday afternoon teachings on meditation. I had no idea what was involved and, with some apprehension, made the one-hour bus trip to attend the first session. I was joined by two of my religious sisters, Lusia from Samoa and Shakuntla from Fiji. The following Saturday we made the same journey and then the next and the next until Father suggested that the 20 or so people attending these sessions form groups in their own areas.

The two sisters and I were the only ones from our area. We had not thought of starting a group but, because of the travel and time involved in reaching the Prayer Centre, responded to the suggestion. Together we discussed the time and venue. The small chapel in our house tends to be noisy at times so we approached the superior of the Marist College at the Pacific Regional Seminary, which is next door to us. Not only were we warmly offered the use of the lovely chapel but Brother Colin sm joined us, becoming a faithful member of the group for the next three years until he was missioned back to Australia.

On Starting a Group

We arranged for a notice to be put in the parish bulletin but weren't expecting much response as we live in a secluded area; few people have cars, the bus service finishes at 6 PM and the time we chose for the meditation was 7:30 PM. With our cassette recorder set the first evening, the four of us had sat down and had begun the session when a taxi drove up and a middle-aged lady with beautiful white hair tiptoed into the chapel. Unfortunately, the taxi reappeared before the session was finished, whisking the lady away. We thought that would be the last time we would see her but she returned the following Thursday with another person.

It turned out that she was a Peace Corps volunteer named Jeanne Jones. As we got to know her, she became a very good friend, introducing other Peace Corps and NGO workers to the group. It slowly grew with several more SMSM sisters, a couple of priests and seminarians and several Fijian ladies who had read the notice in the bulletin joining us. The group still meets weekly and is different from the other groups in Fiji, for it is made up mainly of meditators who are in the country for a certain period of time. Those who have left Fiji have moved on to Japan, Samoa, Kiribati, Australia, Bangkok, Manila, New Zealand and the U.S.A., and most continue along the road of Christian Meditation. I have received many blessings through the bonds established in the group and links are maintained through correspondence. Several days ago I received a letter from Jeanne in Japan thanking me for putting that notice in the parish bulletin several years ago because meditation has become such an important part of her life.

A Path of Faith and Darkness

Christian Meditation has become a very important part of my life, too. It is a path of faith and of darkness but somehow a profound way of entering into an awareness of God, within, at the centre. Before coming to contemplative prayer I would use scripture as my starting-point of my daily morning prayer. When starting out on the path of Christian Meditation I questioned the apparent lack of the use of scripture. However, I now realize that in the practice of meditation I am coming to understand the scriptures with new eyes.

As a member of the Marist Contemplative Community I have the opportunity to be enriched by the daily Office of Readings in the Divine Office. Many times I am struck by the references in scripture, in the writings of the Church Fathers and in spiritual writers to the indwelling presence of Christ and the need for *stillness* in prayer. John Main, in his teaching, is constantly rooting meditation in the words of Jesus and the letters of St. Paul.

There is a poverty intrinsic to Christian Meditation, for I must let go of thoughts and images in order to cross to the silence where God dwells. Through "letting go" in meditation I am slowly and haltingly learning also to let go of anger, animosity and other fixations which are part of my nature. Christian Meditation is the way to freedom, to seeing with Christ's eyes and to journeying along the road begun at baptism to transformation in Christ.

Setting out to Other Cultures

The Constitutions of the Marist Missionary Sisters, the religious family to which I belong, refer to "setting out and setting out again to other cultures and to other peoples" as an integral part of our particular vocation in the church. There is a dying involved in leaving friends, family, an accustomed environment, a lifestyle and ministry for other places and languages which are unfamiliar and in which we operate with clumsiness until we learn the culture and customs.

This process of change and adaptation is a demanding one. The dying and letting go, begun in the prayer of contemplation when we relinquish our thoughts, ideas and images to journey to the centre where God dwells, strengthen us for that part of the journey where we say "yes" to reaching out to peoples of other cultures and societies.

Approximately half the population of this small Pacific island country is native Fijian; the other half comprises mainly the descendants of the Indian indentured workers who were brought to Fiji to work on the sugar cane plantations in the early twentieth century. There is a richness of religious faiths represented by Hindu, Moslem and Sikh groups as well as the different Christian churches. I have often thought how wonderful it would be if we were able to sit down together and meditate in silence, since the spirit of God ultimately reaches beyond all faith traditions and builds bridges of friendship, love, care, reconciliation and understanding.

In our societies today, the family as a social unit is eroding and the forces of consumerism fed by television and videos condition us to believe that happiness is found quickly in the acquisition of material wealth. Being a missionary means leading others to discover that the Spirit of God, who loves each of us unconditionally, dwells within, at the centre. We can have no greater mission than this, but in the proclamation we, too, must be committed to the spiritual pilgrimage.

Chapter 2

The Difficulties of Getting Started

"The Mantra: A Reed Against a Hurricane"

Nina Carpenter

Joe Doerfer

Ed Falchiere

Julie F. Felton

Sheila Geary

Suzy T. Kane

Nina Carpenter

Nina Carpenter worked as an elementary school teacher for many years in eastern Ontario, Canada. Now living in Geneva, Illinois, USA, she recently gave birth to her first child. She comments, "The mantra really did help me calm down when I had moments of panic during labour. It was like a spiritual pacifier."

I know, through my own experience, that the small seed of meditation can grow in spurts, lie dormant and then suddenly grow again when you least expect it. My own dedication to meditation has waxed and waned. Having been prompted many times by various people in different places to follow this spiritual path, I now meditate once a day. My sights are on meditating twice a day. Although I find it difficult to stay focused on the mantra, I feel that my current life is more integrated when I spend time meditating, seeking the quiet, knowing inner presence of God.

Starting to Meditate

My sister first introduced me to meditation in the mid-1980s through a group that meditated in the Avila Center in Thunder Bay, Ontario. Since then I have meditated sporadically. After many changes in my life I ended up living in Ajax, Ontario. It was a particularly stressful and emotionally draining time in my life. I was drawn to a particular parish in Ajax. One day in their bulletin I saw a small two-line ad inviting those interested in Christian Meditation to contact Bill and Sheila Watson. The Watsons lovingly opened their home every week to anyone who wanted to meditate with them. I called and the next week went to meditate with their group.

Again, I only attended the group sporadically but had a developing awareness that this was my lifeline. At this time in my life I felt I was drowning in an ocean, sinking to the bottom, but that someone had cast down an illuminated rope for me to reach and grasp onto. It was leading me gently up out of the cold, dark water. I believe that, through the prayers of my ever-loving mother and family and the discipline of meditation, God had cast a beam of love to save me. After a period of mending my life, I returned to meditate with the Ajax group. At this point, I realized that during the weekly group meetings I could feel the power of two or more being gathered in his name, and this helped my dedication to meditating on my own for the rest of the week.

On Starting a Group

There have been good major changes in my life and I am now living in Geneva, Illinois. I was led to contact Sister Marian McCarthy at the Christian Meditation Center in Roselle, Illinois, and through her found the courage to call around my area to see if anyone was interested in Christian Meditation. Jane Schultz, a very open-minded Director of Adult Education at St. Peter's Parish in Geneva, Illinois, agreed to give it a try. Since October 1996 we have been meeting weekly in the church rectory or other meeting rooms. We have had to change our time and location, working around basketball practices and violin lessons, but we have a core group of three or four people who come fairly regularly, with other people floating in and out. We welcome anyone to our meeting with open hearts and have recently had a few newcomers drop in.

Forming this group was important to me because meditating with others supports me in innumerable ways. Recently, one woman in the group made a short but revealing statement that she was in the midst of dealing with unexpected changes in her life which she felt were beyond her influence and control. She realized that during these times of stress she was tempted to give up meditating, when paradoxically she needed to meditate the most. Her insight was like a gift being presented to me on a silver platter. I related immediately to what she said and felt more understanding and compassion for both her situation and my own, and for our shared humanity.

In the Abyss, the Face of God

Meditating is sometimes like leaning over the edge of our hectic and noise-filled days to peer into the still waters of the abyss. It's a sight that is not only peaceful in its own right but also illuminates by reflecting back into our awareness the debris that needs to be removed so that we can feel the joy of living in the present moment, day by day. In the silence of meditating together and in the short comments we share before or after our meditation, I find the courage and security to recognize, in the abyss, the face of God.

In light of my own vacillation I would urge anyone who has ignored or forgotten that the seeds of contemplation lie within ourselves to find God in the garden of meditation. Feeling scared or apprehensive about this invitation may be a sign that the seeds indeed will bear fruit in you. I know from my experience that the gift is waiting there with many blessings. The seeds have been planted; now is the time to cultivate them.

Joe Doerfer

Joe Doerfer, of Tucson, Arizona, USA, is married with four children and eight grandchildren. Retired, he now manages Medio-Media, the publishing arm of the World Community for Christian Meditation, and has recently started a meditation group in Tucson.

Catholic schools in the mid-1940s to mid-1950s formed my religious beliefs. Priests and sisters taught Catholic doctrine from the Baltimore Catechism. Sisters complained to my parents that I was always wiggling in my seat and did not concentrate. I was a shy, skinny kid without an ounce of self-confidence. Not surprisingly, I received poor grades and was constantly on the brink of failing.

My faith, however, was strong. I attended Mass daily and never missed Tuesday night Mother of Perpetual Help Devotions. I sat in the hard pews, viewing the back of many heads, waiting to go to confession each Saturday afternoon. Many days I served Mass for a retired monsignor at 5:30 AM, and then attended Mass later in the day with the school. It was an immature faith but a faith strongly felt.

Faith and the Unconditional Love of God

All of this faith was destroyed by an immature act. I shoplifted a flashlight from a neighbourhood hardware store. It was one of those events in your life you never forget. In my mind's eye I can still picture that flashlight. It was army green and could be clipped to a belt. I found myself in a trap that I could not get myself out of. Confession, which before was part of my life, changed to a process that scared and confused me. The parish priest would draw a round circle on the blackboard and fill it with white chalk. Each venial sin would erase a little of the white soul but a mortal sin would erase all of the white, just leaving a black soul. Afraid to confess my black mortal sin, I skipped Saturday afternoon confession.

Not wanting everyone to know that I had committed a mortal sin, I felt I had to take communion. How demeaning it would be to stand alone as everyone else was filing out of the pew to receive communion. Now of course I had committed another mortal sin. I certainly could not confess that I received communion in sin. This began a spiral that spun me away from my faith. I began later to question and doubt the faith that made up my religious tradition. I have since then rebelled against dogma that defines belief absolutely without leaving room for the unconditional love of God.

Power, Money and Giving up Meditation

Concentration has continued to be a problem. I have many interests but find it hard to remain with any one subject long enough to become competent. This lack of commitment also described my religious path. Many books about Eastern and Western meditation and philosophy sit on my bookshelf, read but not assimilated. I was introduced to Transcendental Meditation (TM) some 25 years ago to help me deal with stress. I practised TM for five years and then slipped back into the world of job promotions, power and money. I eventually gave up meditation.

This lifestyle resulted in a heart attack and bypass surgery. After recovering from that significant moment I began looking again for an answer to change my life. I then picked up the book *The Good Heart,* thinking it was something to do with the physical heart. The book, however, was a narration of the John Main Seminar that featured the Dalai Lama commenting on the Christian scriptures. I was led to find out more about the World Community for Christian Meditation, the organization that was open enough to bring the Buddhist and Christian traditions together.

Beginning the Pilgrimage

The idea of a Christian mantra was attractive because of my background. After reading and listening to tapes by Fr. John Main and Fr. Laurence Freeman, I was exhilarated by the possibility of getting in touch with my real self and experiencing the love of God living in my heart. To go beyond thinking, language, judging and dogma by just simply concentrating on the mantra was not just a way, but *the way for me.*

In the beginning my teacher had to be from the books and tapes of Fr. John and Fr. Laurence. There wasn't a meditation group in Tucson, Arizona. Encouragement from the weekly Internet meditation reading transcribed by Carla Cooper and created and maintained by Greg Ryan became my meditation group. Now, however, after starting a group in my parish, I have 12 fellow meditators with whom to share and grow. I am looking forward to a long and fruitful exposure to the World Community of Christian Meditation.

Ed Falchiere

Ed Falchiere lives in the Bronx, New York, USA, with his wife Deborah and their children Marni and Ian. He is a clinical social worker who directs a program for adolescents at a private psychiatric hospital. Ed has led a meditation group at the Church of St. Michael the Archangel in the Co-op City section of the Bronx since 1992.

My first encounter with Christian Meditation was at a weekend workshop given by Fr. Laurence Freeman at the New York Open Center in August 1987. I had been on a spiritual-metaphysical path for some time before the workshop, but found myself feeling dissatisfied with my tendency to intellectualize my spiritual journey.

At a time when I felt a strong need for a deeper experience, I came across a description in the Open Center catalogue of a Christian Meditation workshop given by Fr. Laurence. I wasn't particularly centred in my Catholic identity, and so I entered the workshop with some skepticism. I was pleasantly surprised by the experience. I liked Fr. Laurence. I liked what he had to say about John Main's teaching on meditation and I was comfortable with his use of metaphysical language. Until that time I had never heard a priest speak of such concepts as the ego, the true self and the world of illusion.

I Hated the Practice of Meditation

There was just one problem; I hated the *practice* of meditation! During the weekend I found myself feeling unsettled by it and resisting it. I clearly remember leaving the workshop feeling frustrated and asking God, "Why did you send me here? What was all this for?" Of course the answer to my questions was not apparent then. Later it became clear to me that a seed had been planted and the process of becoming a meditator had begun.

As the months passed, I still felt this restless need for something deeper and so I dabbled with other kinds of meditation. Yet it was as though God kept tapping me on the shoulder and pointing me back towards Christian Meditation. After several such taps, I decided to get some books by John Main. This turned out to be helpful but I was still not off and running. Indeed, as with most meditators, there were several false starts. Finally, a few years after the workshop, I took the plunge and began the twice-daily journey of meditation.

On Meditating in a Car

Although I did not belong to a group during my first two years of meditating, I received much support from reading and rereading John Main's *Moment of Christ* and listening to his taped talks from *In the Beginning*. My early morning meditation, before my young children were awake, was relatively easy to do, but I felt I needed to be creative with my second meditation, when they were up and about. So determined was I to get in my second meditation that I would meditate (albeit self-consciously) in my car, parked in our garage complex, when I arrived home from work. This went on for some time until one evening an elderly woman tapped on my window to ask if I was okay, no doubt wondering if I had expired. It was then that I decided to accommodate my second meditation at home.

The Next Step: Starting a Group

After meditating for two years, I began to feel a need to be part of a meditation group. Since there were no groups near my home, I decided to start one of my own, not knowing when or how I could do it. It happened that on the day I registered my family at the Church of St. Michael the Archangel in Co-op City, I decided to mention to Sr. Ann, the pastoral associate, my involvement with Christian Meditation and the teaching of John Main. To my surprise, she told me that not only had she known of John Main but that there had been a Christian Meditation group in that parish until a year before. Apparently the group ended when the priest who led it had moved on. With such a precedent, I quickly received the church's support in starting a group.

When the group first began there were usually three or four of us at our weekly meeting, and for a long time I was the only man in the group. Things began to change, however, when in December 1992 St. Michael's moved from its storefront premises to a beautiful contemporary church. It was at this time that the group began to draw more interest, often just by word of mouth. Like most groups, we have gone through a series of expansions and contractions, but we continue to have a faithful core membership. Although we have had our share of people who have come and gone, they have enriched the group even in their passing through.

What is particularly interesting about our group is the great diversity of its membership. This is reflective of Co-op City, the world's largest residential cooperative and its surrounding area. Our group has welcomed Black, White and Latino men and women, ranging in age from young adults to senior citizens. In addition to those members who come from our parish, others have come from Pentecostal and Protestant churches as well as from Jewish and Islamic backgrounds. Others have no particular religious ties but come with a great spiritual hunger.

Our group has also attracted people from Alcoholics Anonymous. While everyone in the group brings unique gifts to it, those who have come from this 12-step program often bring a special enthusiasm and energy. As Fr. Laurence once suggested to me, people such as these have come to a real poverty of spirit in their lives and therefore approach meditation with a great openness for healing.

Just as the experience of meditation has been a gift in our lives, so too has the experience of meeting as a group. The group has provided each of us with support and love on what would otherwise be a solitary spiritual path. In a way, the group parallels the individual meditative journey in that we have persevered through the years with no expectations except to *be* with each other.

The Journey into the Unknown

If anyone had told me when I walked out of that workshop in the summer of 1987 that I would eventually become a faithful meditator and that I would be leading a meditation group, I would not have believed them. Yet God works in mysterious ways. As I look back at my initial resistance to meditation, I can see that fear was at work. I must have sensed that I was opening a door which would lead me on a journey of great significance. It was a journey into the unknown and so I resisted. Thankfully, the Holy Spirit gently led me back to that now-opened door, guided me through it and showed me there is nothing to fear.

My intuition that something of ultimate importance was happening through meditation is something that once scared me, but now sustains me. I sense this no matter how the meditation is going, no matter how distracted I may be. I have learned that, as long as I meditate in good faith and I keep returning to the mantra whenever I'm distracted, my heart continues to open and the pilgrimage to the centre of my being progresses.

Julie F. Felton

Julie Felton was born and grew up in Sutton, Surrey, England. She has been married to her husband, Don, for over 40 years and they live in Sacramento, California, USA. They have four adult children (a son and three daughters) and at last count five grandsons and two granddaughters.

My story begins in 1990, when I arrived home in California from England, after spending six weeks with my 90-year-old mother before she died. She was a very warm, sparkling lady with perfect makeup, manicured nails and silver hair. She had a tremendous sense of fun and loved life and people. She was the kind of person whom all her family and friends couldn't imagine living without, and the loss was very painful. I had dealt with the details of her funeral and had settled my brother, who was in his fifties, slightly developmentally disabled and living alone in the family home in England.

Upon my return home, my husband drew attention to a notice in our parish church bulletin offering a three-day silent meditation retreat at Three Rivers, California, a little place in the foothills almost two hours' drive north from where we lived. He urged me to go, feeling sure it was just what I needed to help the healing process take place. I called our parish office and learned that only one woman wanted to go and she needed a ride! Although I was exhausted, I reluctantly agreed to drive.

Screaming Monkey Voices

The talk the first evening, by Fr. Laurence Freeman, explained why we meditate and how we meditate. I thought he was crazy expecting that kind of time commitment. He was, in my opinion, definitely not in touch with how real people live in the real world. I like to go to daily Mass; my doctor says I have to exercise; the dermatologist says I have to take care of sun-damaged skin; my dentist says I have to floss my teeth! Unless you start work at noon, we are talking about serious sleep deprivation here if you are to do all this in one day. Impossible! Then we had the first meditation period and all the "screaming monkey voices" began in my head. It felt more like three hours than half an hour; I relived in that time every competent and incompetent thing I had ever said or done.

I also found I had stopped saying the proper mantra, the word "Ma-ra-na-tha," and I had begun saying "marinara"! I asked myself, "How long have you been praying about pasta sauce?" (A joke my darling mother would have dearly loved.) This was definitely not for me!

I went back to my room and a huge sadness overwhelmed me. I thought about my husband at home alone after all my time away in England. I thought about my brother trying to cope alone in an unkind, scary world, thousands of miles away from me. I thought about my mother's death and I cried. Completely exhausted, I fell asleep determined to find a ride home for my companion and to leave after breakfast the next morning.

Morning Has Broken

I awoke in time for the early meditation period feeling strangely rested and more peaceful, even after so few hours' sleep. At morning prayer they played "Morning Has Broken" by Eleanor Farjeon (1881–1965). It had been one of my mother's favourites; I had chosen it for her funeral and it felt like she was again right there talking to me. Even the meditation period seemed more peaceful and as I relaxed, I felt moments of true stillness. By now, deep down I knew I had to stay. I still didn't like it but I felt for some reason I was meant to be there. Boris Pasternak once said, "When a great moment knocks on the door of your life, very often it is no louder than a heartbeat, so unless you are paying careful attention it is easy to miss it." This felt like one of those moments.

I was a reluctant meditator for about two years, stopping and starting again. It felt a bit like beginning a new exercise regimen, when you hate every minute of it but know it is good for you. My husband and I had three temporary residences hundreds of miles apart; we were sorting out several very exciting, successful businesses we owned and the California economy prevented us from selling anything and changing our lifestyle. Roots are very important to me, but we had no real roots. By this time I was in a serious depression. Trying to find the right doctors and medications when I was lost, confused and "running on empty" was very painful and I was hospitalized briefly, which was agony for my husband.

It is encouraging to note that three psychiatrists in different cities and two therapists all urged me to continue meditating! My husband, who doesn't meditate, credits meditation with substantially improving my mental health. With a brilliant therapist, hard work and time, I healed. We sold our houses in Los Angeles and Bakersfield, California, and settled in a beautiful house in Sacramento, California.

The Guidance of the Spirit

I have felt the Holy Spirit's guidance repeatedly as I have sought to simplify my life in as many areas as possible. We still travel for business and pleasure and to visit our children and all those wonderful grandbabies. However, I have tried to ground myself as much as possible and invite silence into my life at every opportunity. I check the "plethora of images," to use an expression of Fr. John

Main, that comes into my life and gently and lovingly create for myself a more peaceful environment within which to live and work.

I started two Christian Meditation groups at my home in the fall of 1996. I offer one on Monday evenings, hoping to attract working people, but so far this group is struggling. The Tuesday morning group flourishes with between four and eight meditators attending. I try to create a welcoming, peaceful setting for the group, and this in turn creates some very prayerful moments for me during the preparation. Whatever work has to be done before the meditation group meeting I try to do gently, usually to soft classical music. We follow the recommended format, listening to a teaching tape by either Fr. John or Fr. Laurence. We enjoy some soft music to take away the words and then meditate for 25 minutes, ending with soft music. We allow time for questions or comments and, although it is not a social time and I don't even serve refreshments, we have formed a very strong caring bond between us. We part company each week strengthened by the group and we hate to miss a gathering.

I still visit my brother in the little village of Emsworth in Hampshire each summer, helping him keep his life on track. It amazed me to find a meditation group right there in the village. I try to attend when I am there. All of this helps to keep me grounded in the practice of meditation.

I try to look at each day as a clean canvas, no matter how hectic and busy it is, and to remember that I am the artist: I hold the brush and I choose the colours. Sometimes I am tired, confused and distracted when I return to my "journey," the work of meditation, of saying my mantra. At other times I am rested, focused and peaceful and my twice-daily meditation washes over me like a gentle spring rain.

Peace that Surpasses All Understanding

As with most people, meditation turned my prayer life upside down. It has also influenced the rest of my life, my direction, my focus, my priorities. In return it has given me a confidence that I am where I ought to be, doing what I ought to be doing, on a path God wants me to follow and finding "a peace that surpasses all understanding."

Sheila Geary

Sheila Geary, 44, is a writer living in Madison, Wisconsin, USA. Her first career was in advertising and publishing, mostly in Chicago. After she left, and after a brief stint as a cab driver in her Florida home town, she returned to Chicago to study graduate-level film and video for two years. She is currently writing a book telling the story of her father's death and the profound effect it has had on her and her large Irish-Catholic family.

I read recently that we don't turn to God until we need him. That was the case with me. I was raised by good parents who taught me about God through their daily lives, but still I grew up feeling alone. I rejected everything about religion as soon as I got to college. My first career was in advertising, a world where my fierce ambition to be someone was fuelled by the glamour, money and perceived status of the industry. I found the climb intoxicating, the frenetic 60-hour work weeks and pressure all-encompassing and wonderfully pain-numbing.

I ended up on Wall Street 10 years later, and it was here that I could finally admit my life wasn't working. The pain of shallow living was unbearable by now, and I knew if I wasn't happy here, at "the top," I never would be. I had no clue where to turn so I just left New York, wandering around for nine months, finally ending up back in my home town, completely broke, totally lost. Unbeknownst to me and my horrified family, I had begun to make my way toward an authentic life.

The Mantra: A Reed Against a Hurricane

As these things happen, Fr. Laurence Freeman came to town around that time and I went to hear about meditation (it having been deemed "hip"). I remember how, in the beginning, I could hardly bear to do the whole 20 minutes. I constantly had to will myself to stay in one position. My mind was run over with long-repressed anger and gyrating thoughts, and the mantra seemed to be a reed against a hurricane. But I persisted, believing Fr. Laurence when he told us that total commitment was absolutely necessary, and I clung to the words he read to us from St. Paul: "He who calls you is to be trusted. He will do it."

Mostly, though, I hung in there because I felt acutely the humility, intelligence and peace of Fr. Laurence's presence. Spiritually-connected people have a power that is the opposite of that of worldly, successful people, and the difference has always struck me in the deepest part of my being where my ego isn't in charge. I knew he had what I sought; if he said meditation was the key, then I was going to try and use it.

I've been meditating twice a day for seven years now and, as promised, my life has changed. I support myself with "ordinary" jobs today, allowing myself space to work at my writing. I'm living in a small town close to cows and sheep. And I'm so much happier. It occurred to me recently that my meditation periods are like stretching in the morning, a way of unknotting my mind, of becoming limber, so I can absorb organically all that will come along that day, "good" and "bad."

Meditation Is My Connector

This week I've experienced great frustration with a powerful computer I have and don't understand, and I'm being told that its pathways are not connecting properly. Meditation is my connector: left to my own devices, I would return again and again to my old way of living, of trying to control uncontrollable circumstances, determining the course of my life based on my relentless desires for security and approval. Now when I recognize I've reverted to that way of being and feel discouraged about it, just knowing I'm a meditator who can return to the source helps me to calm down and be gentler with myself.

It's a sneaky thing, this practice of meditation. If Fr. Laurence had told me in the beginning that if I was faithful to it, I would begin to live the gospel, or at least want to try and live it, I'm sure I would have gotten up and left the room. But he didn't say that; instead he talked of authentic living, of silence as an aligning balm, and of peace. So it has crept up on me, this love and compassion for others. Significantly, I've also grown more loving toward my own self, my true self, whom I ignored before all this started.

Suzy T. Kane

Suzy Kane lives with her husband, Tom, in Bedford Hills, New York, USA; they have two grown sons. She is a professional writer currently working on a book The Hidden History of the Persian Gulf War. *Suzy wrote a thesis for a Master's degree at Manhattanville College on George Bush and the Gulf War and has had many letters and articles on war and peace issues printed in a variety of publications including* The New York Times, Time *magazine and* The Washington Post.

During three different one-month stays over the course of several years, St. Mary's Convent in Peekskill, New York, generously provided me with the "solitude in community" I needed to work on a difficult writing project. My husband, Tom, recognizing my battle with the constant interruptions that normally beset an office in the home, was also generously willing to hold the fort while I retreated.

A contemplative order of Episcopalian nuns (who wear the traditional navy habit), the sisters of St. Mary's, structure their day around the Divine Office. Although I was baptized Catholic but raised in the Dutch Reformed Church, I felt welcome at St. Mary's. So while staying at the convent, I too rose at 4:45 each morning in time for Matins and Mass in the chapel. After silent breakfast I returned to my room, where I worked at my desk until Sext at noon. After the silent midday dinner, I took a half-hour walk along a path with scenic views of the Hudson River to air out my lungs and brain and stretch my legs. Before I settled back down to work around 2 PM, I sometimes stopped in to browse the walk-in closet the sisters had converted to a bookstore they stocked for guests and retreatants. I resumed work until 5:20 PM, when I stopped to attend Vespers followed by silent supper (Sunday was "talking" supper, but having become used to silence, when Sunday came, I found I did not have much to say!).

To keep my body from assuming the shape of a chair, I often did yoga exercises in my room during the interval between supper and Compline at 8:05. Returning to my room from Compline, I showered and readied for bed, sitting back down at my computer for an hour or so if my work was going well, or getting into bed to read before shutting off the light. This was my daily discipline for what I called my "month of Sundays."

John Main's The Heart of Creation

It was in the little convent bookstore in February 1990 that I picked up a copy of *The Heart of Creation* and met John Main. Having made friends with silence at St. Mary's, you might say I was ready to meet John Main. ("When the student is ready, the teacher arrives.") I was tired of always reading *about* spiritual experience; I wanted to experience it, to *do* something, to have something happen. I was not initially attracted to the idea of saying a mantra, in particular a strange word like *Maranatha*, so at first I tried just peering into the blackness, listening in the dark without a mantra for five minutes in the afternoon four days in a row. At the time, five minutes seemed long. But then, as I got deeper into reading John Main, I decided to follow his simple instructions of using the mantra, and trying to stay with it for at least 20 minutes, I discovered I could.

My Mind Kept Wandering

It was not easy to repeat the word *Maranatha* because my mind kept wandering, but as Main suggests, I learned to gently pull it back with the mantra. I began to understand the meaning of "active passivity." Sometimes I preface my meditation with a few minutes of reading of John Main, Laurence Freeman (whom I got to hear on his last trip to New York City), the Bible, or some other inspirational Christian, Buddhist or Sufi writing. When I returned to civilian life, my routine of meditating 20 minutes in the morning and 20 minutes in the evening became my "Home Office."

After almost six years of faithfully meditating twice a day, however, the first interruption in my routine came when I was hospitalized with a ruptured appendix. (An emergency appendectomy is no excuse to stop meditating! I know that because John Main faithfully meditated all through his bout with cancer right up to his death.) Although I am well again, my recovery took much longer than I expected because of complications that twice put me back in the hospital. I do believe that rerouting some of my meditation time for visualization exercises, though, helped me heal.

Giving up on Morning Meditation

But once I had broken my stride, it became easier to give up my morning meditation for a few weeks because... well, I did not know why. Nothing seemed to be happening in my meditation, it was true, but I was not supposed to be expecting anything to happen in the first place, was I? I was discouraged by the seeming fruitlessness of meditation, but my newfound 20 minutes to linger over my morning coffee and *The New York Times* were not satisfying either. Paradoxically, by not meditating in the morning, I felt I had less time than ever.

Six years to the month of meeting John Main and beginning my discipline of meditation, I attended a weekend silent retreat at St. Mary's, which I had not visited for a couple of years. The priest who led the retreat decided at the last minute to change his topic to "Centering Prayer." This contemplative practice is somewhat similar to that described by John Main and was developed by Fr. Thomas Keating, a Cistercian priest and monk at St. Benedict's Monastery in Snowmass, Colorado (where my husband and I were headed the very next week!). I learned that it is common while meditating to feel in a fog, as I did, in which nothing seems to be happening. Some experience this as a "dry" period.

A Cloud Covers the Mountain

During the retreat, I was struck at Mass by the synchronistic readings in Exodus (24:12, 16-18) about Moses on the mountain. Those of us familiar with the story know that Moses is going to come down the mountain with the stone tablets on which are written God's law and commandments. But as Moses ascends the mountain, he does not know that! A cloud is covering the mountain, and God calls to Moses from "inside the cloud." Not knowing what he was getting into, Moses, the model for all meditators, courageously climbs "right into the cloud," the "cloud of unknowing." The retreat helped me look in a new way at my own fog in meditating.

Now on those occasions when I am tempted to skip meditation, I remind myself of the scene in the garden of Gethsemane, where Jesus asked such a seemingly small thing of his friends: to stay awake with him while he prayed. Of course they let him down by falling asleep. Because I know the story, I can imagine how ashamed I would be to hear the voice of such a dear friend: "What! Could you not watch with me 20 minutes?" And so I watch for 20 minutes in the morning and 20 minutes in the evening, even though sometimes I admit I do not have a generosity of spirit in reporting for what often seems like duty. At the end of each 20 minutes, however, I am always glad I did meditate. Maybe someday I will better understand *why*.

Chapter 3

On Trying Different Traditions of Meditation

"The Search Is On"

Joseph L. Barcello
Dorothy Deakin
Lionel E. Goulet
Pat Kasmarik
James Logan
William Mishler
Isobel Page
Jo Russell
Frank Seeburger

Joseph L. Barcello

Joseph Barcello lives with his wife, Angie, in their home on Terrible Mountain, Vermont, USA; they have six children. Their practice of meditation has been formed by John Main and Thich Nhat Hanh, as well as by other spiritual teachers from both the East and the West. They have led a Christian Meditation group in their 35-acre retreat for the past eight years. Joe recently entered the lay chaplaincy program at a Medical Centre in New Hampshire.

My interest in meditation began many years ago. Literature on meditation was very scarce then, and I did not know anyone who meditated. I tried different methods, going from one method to another. It was discouraging, but the desire to meditate stayed with me.

It seemed that at the time there were two choices for people who wanted to meditate. One choice was the Western concept of discursive meditation, where we would read a passage from scripture or take a theme and dwell on that using thoughts and images. The other was the silent way of the East, which seemed mysterious and exotic. I was drawn to the Eastern way of meditating and made many starts at it. I failed as many times. I tried learning on my own with the meagre amount of literature that was available. I never felt satisfied. I did not know then that satisfaction should not be a goal and should not even be desired.

The Montreal Priory

Eventually I did meet people who meditated. Two of them, who were friends of mine, introduced me to the Montreal Benedictine Priory where Christian meditation was practised and taught. They encouraged me to make a retreat there, and the idea appealed to me. When I called to register, the secretary asked if I was familiar with John Main's writings. When I told her that I was not, she suggested I read two of his books before starting the retreat. One was *Christian Meditation: The Gethsemani Talks*. The other was *Word into Silence*. It was there that I got a good grounding in meditation as it was taught by John Main, who had learned to meditate from a Hindu Swami. This was what I was looking for.

The Practice of Zen Buddhism

My first glimpse of another Eastern tradition was at a Christian–Buddhist retreat given by a Catholic monk of the Carthusian order. He had studied in Burma and returned to the United States from time to time to give workshops and retreats. He taught insight meditation (Vipassana) and complemented it with the Christian teaching. After this exposure to Buddhism, I made a *metta* (Pali word for loving-kindness) retreat at the Insight Meditation Society, a Buddhist retreat centre in Barre, Massachusetts. In reading much of the writing of the Vietnamese Zen master and poet Thich Nhat Hanh, I was inspired to want to experience the practice of Zen Buddhism firsthand. I did that at the Zen Mountain Monastery in Mount Tremper, New York.

While I explore Buddhism I can say, as William Johnston, S.J., says in his book *Letters to Contemplatives*, "I put my roots more and more deeply into the Bible and the Christian tradition while remaining open to the dharma and wisdom of the eastern teachers."

The journey for me has been and still is very exciting. I find myself searching and not resting in one place for very long. John Main said, "No matter how long we have been meditating, we are always beginners." I find that to be very true, and I believe this adds to the excitement and the fervour of the journey.

On Starting a Meditation Group

When I began meditating in the way taught by John Main, one of the two friends who introduced me to the Montreal Priory suggested that I start a meditation group in my area. The idea seemed quite farfetched and I quickly rejected it. The suggestion, however, stayed with me and, after praying and pondering on it for about a year, I decided to see if there was enough interest among my friends to begin a group. There was immediate enthusiasm.

We formed a group in the summer of 1989 and have been meeting weekly ever since. During some of those years my wife and I had a guest house and would house people visiting the Weston Priory, a Benedictine monastery located a few minutes away in Weston, Vermont. We would invite our guests to meditate with our group, which meets on Thursday nights. Many people were introduced to meditation on those nights and some later formed their own groups in their home states.

With meditating and living here in the beautiful Green Mountains of Vermont, we must be alert and conscious of keeping the beauty of both fresh and alive. They are both gifts.

Dorothy Deakin

Dorothy Deakin is a retired pioneer Speech/Language Pathologist living in Kelowna, British Columbia, Canada. While living in England she studied Philosophy with the School of Economic Science, a branch of a school founded by the Russian philosopher P.D. Ouspensky. She was initiated in 1960 into meditation in the Advaita Tradition of the Hindu Sanatan Dharma, the non-dual Perennial Philosophy, the same tradition that Dom John Main met in Kuala Lumpur. Dorothy is also the Canadian representative of the Study Society – the society for the study of normal psychology in London, England. She holds weekly Advaita meditation and study meetings in Kelowna, B.C., and is a regular participant at a Christian Meditation group there. She has experienced a greater understanding and a deepening of her Christian faith as a result of her involvement in the Eastern tradition and looks forward to the day when the commonalities of all the world's religions will be fully realized by humankind everywhere in the cosmic Christ.

When I first stepped onto the path of my spiritual pilgrimage I was offered a choice of two goals. One was integrality and the other was to give service. It was understood that integrality was the superior of the two and so, being an ambitious young woman, I chose that one, although I am certain now that I did not know what it meant.

A few years later, while living in England and active in a school of Philosophy, I was instructed in a method of meditation. A few days after receiving this gift, during a half-hour meditation, I must have gone very deep beyond the mantra; I have no idea for how long. When I "came to" I felt a strange stillness and peace, and wondered where I had been for that time. I knew I had not been asleep. St. John of the Cross described this state very well when he said, "I entered in, I know not where, transcending knowledge with my thought," only I had had no thought.

I arose and got a cup of tea. It had been raining and the sun was beginning to come out. As I went towards the glass French doors everything inside the room and outside was suddenly illuminated by an other-worldly brilliance and I knew that I was bathed in this same light. At the same time I was vaguely aware of the neighbour's Siamese cat running over the lawn, and even of a puff of smoke from a train passing behind the trees. The mantra was going on and on and on in my head as if bathing everything within my vision, and me, with the sacred word. I also realized that the word being repeated was an Eastern name of God and it was imperative that I should know that God is all and that there is no separation between God and the universe and myself. I knew without any uncertainty that all is perfect unity. I was engulfed by love and overpowered by gratitude and fell to my knees as tears of joy flowed from my eyes. I have no idea how long this lasted. I felt very humbled afterwards by the grace of such an experience.

I returned to Canada in 1964 to pioneer speech therapy in the interior of British Columbia, and to rejoin a philosophy study group to which I had belonged before going to England nine years earlier. I met with considerable hostility from the group leader concerning my studies and experiences in England. These experiences were completely invalidated and I was ordered not to meditate any more.

I felt as though a vital part of my life had been cut off. For almost three years I was not aware that I was slowly being brainwashed, as my mind and soul became more and more the object of possession by this teacher. I knew nothing of cults, but somehow in December 1967 I found the courage to sever the relationship.

For the next two-and-a-half months I received threatening letters and telephone calls warning me of the dangers that would ensue. Because of the brainwashing, I more than half believed all this. And then, in early February, after the most damaging letter, I received a phone call in which I was told that I was doomed to suffer terribly for the rest of my life and every life thereafter, and there was nothing that I could do to prevent it.

During the next few days I came very close to suicide. I felt that I had nothing left to live for. I began to write a cry for help to a friend who was a clergyman. As I began to write I felt utter poverty. I had nothing that could help me. Suddenly a voice from inside me said very strongly, "You have the meditation, no one can take that away from you!" I began to repeat the mantra. As it started to find its own rhythm, the word changed and I realized that I was listening over and over to these words of Julian of Norwich: "All shall be well and all shall be well, and all manner of things shall be well."

The words went on and on and seemed to fill my whole being. Suddenly I realized that I was forgiven – forgiven for allowing myself to be forced to stop meditating and for the whole of the past three years. With the realization that I was forgiven there also came the knowledge that I must completely forgive my teacher.

As in the previous experience, I was engulfed by love. I felt certain that nothing and no one would ever be able to hurt me. The tensions of the past few years poured out of me in floods of tears, not of sadness but of gratitude and pure bliss. I knew it was true that nothing could ever separate me from the love of God. I knew this was a moment of divine grace.

Four days later I received a letter from a friend I had known in the school of philosophy. She had been going down the long flight of stairs in the building where they held meetings, and something had said to her, "That Canadian girl who used to drive you home is in great trouble. Write to her at once." She did, and later when I asked her how she knew, her reply was, "Well, isn't that unity? When the big toe gets stepped on, the whole body feels the pain."

I never heard from my ex-teacher again. I did visit her in hospital later when she was seriously ill and told her I had forgiven her and asked her to forgive me for any distress that I might have caused her. She turned her face to the wall. Her priest urged her to forgive so that she could die in peace but she refused. It had been she who had originally given me the choice between the goal of integrality or of service. I have to remember to thank God for her putting me on the path of my pilgrimage in the first place.

I believe that I have learned what integrality means. It is more than integrity, which is mostly concerned with wholeness and completeness within an individual and which usually has a good effect on one's relationships with others. Integrality is also wholeness and completeness, but in which the individual has the direct experience of oneness with God and the universe. It is the experience wherein God is revealed as the source of love and the source of life and the ground of all being. If this is so, then integrality leads the individual into service, the kind of service which springs from humility and love and of which St. Paul says, "Now not I, but Christ lives in me," and of which Pope John XXIII said, "I am nothing." Then the service to others, wholeheartedly committed, risky though it may be, is the mark of the validity of the experience.

Lionel E. Goulet

Lionel E. Goulet lives in Toronto, Ontario, Canada. A McGill University Law School graduate, he recently retired as Product Manager of corporate and securities law products of a worldwide legal publishing firm.

He practised many forms of meditation until he discovered native spirituality and the practice of Christian Meditation. Lionel is a Benedictine oblate of Christ the King Monastery, London, England, and has a number of hobbies including genealogical research, antique book collecting and the study of ancient Mayan civilization.

Now that I have achieved "codgerhood," I reflect on my spiritual journey, which I believe began in an early childhood experience. In the early 1930s, when I was about four years old, our family lived in a log cabin on a farm in southern Manitoba. I can remember to this day visiting my father, who was helping with the harvest on my grandfather's farm.

I recall the state of childish joy of running through high autumn grass and golden wheatfields to see my father, who was seated high on a hay rick, driving a team of horses. There was the sound of meadowlarks and crickets on that sunny autumn day. I felt that I had an infinite number of such days ahead of me. I could not resist the feeling that I was part of nature and that nature was good.

The next step on my spiritual journey was attending a Jesuit high school in Winnipeg, where I was taught Ignatian spirituality. Years later, I was to meditate with Anthony de Mello, S.J., learning his Sadhanna techniques. From there, I went to university in Montreal and was introduced to Zen Meditation in a comparative course. The Zen master who taught Zen meditation in Montreal later opened a Zen temple 15 minutes from my home in Toronto.

It must be noted that this journey along the meditative highway using various techniques was not a promiscuous grazing at the spiritual smorgasbord, but took place at different times over a 30-year span.

In Toronto, in 1980, I was attracted to Christian Meditation by a notice in a Catholic newspaper announcing that John Main was coming to teach meditation at the Newman Centre. I have been practising Christian Meditation ever since that course. It was through Christian Meditation that my journey took an unexpected turn.

Born a Half-breed and a Métis

It started through genealogical research that I was conducting for a family reunion, wherein I discovered that I had native-Canadian ancestors. I was both a half-breed and a Métis. It was a great surprise to discover that my siblings and I were direct descendants of Louis Hébert, a herbalist who was the first apothecary and first white farmer in New France. Historical records show that he learned much of his skill as a farmer from the native farmers of Nova Scotia and Quebec. He was also a confidant of Samuel de Champlain.

Shortly after that, in June 1996, a notice arrived in the mail announcing that the North Bay Christian Meditators were holding a seminar at the Anishinabe Spirituality Centre in northern Ontario. That centre is run by the Jesuits. So, I felt right at home: a Jesuit institution hosting a Christian Meditation seminar on native spirituality.

Native Spirituality and Meditation

Let me tell you about some of the events that took place at the seminar and what I learned from them. A native religious sister who practised Christian Meditation gave a talk outlining the many similarities between native spirituality and Christian Meditation. A native elder explained the mysteries of the medicine wheel (for "medicine" read "power"). She also conducted a sunrise ceremony on a cold summer morning. It was interesting to see about 60 seminar participants from towns in the area and from Ottawa and Toronto (incidentally both native Canadian names) standing in a circle, listening to chants and inhaling the scent of burning sweetgrass. The seminar returned me to my roots and renewed my reverence for nature.

At the end of the seminar, we city folks went away energized. I often observed that when my coworkers in a modern publishing office went wilderness camping, golfing, skiing, or walking in the woods, they returned refreshed. I feel that this energy came from their direct contact with nature, a contact we have lost or minimized because we have insulated ourselves from nature by our use of cement and steel. We walk on paved sidewalks, live in highrise apartment buildings and work in skyscrapers, distant from *terra firma*. City dwellers live in a cement desert that is often dull, dirty and dangerous, where many of the inhabitants are in a *coma* of the heart (i.e., lacking in compassion) and suffering from *glaucoma* of the soul (i.e., a diminished spiritual vision).

Desert in the City

But wait! I learned to meditate in large cities. And, as Carlo Carreto wrote, the word "desert" means more than a geographical location. After all, the desert was where the desert monks withdrew to meditate. I found that a city can have quiet places to which ordinary people can withdraw to find God in silence and prayer. If I cannot go to the desert, then the desert must come to me. In other words, let us make a desert in the city, in the heart of crowded places. The sages tell us that the time to begin meditation is *now*, whatever our physical and mental state happens to be.

In the Centre Exists Reality

At the seminar, I learned that the medicine wheel is a symbol of great antiquity used by many of the aboriginals of the world. Apparently, NASA photographs of North America reveal that there is a trail of medicine wheels from northern Alberta, Canada, right into South America. The wheel in native spirituality expresses concepts in four equal segments. The units can be the four cardinal directions, the four seasons, the races of the world, or four aspects of human nature: physical, mental, emotional and spiritual. As we walk around the circle, we must develop each aspect equally, or else we will live in a state of disharmony. Our goal is to reach the centre, wherein harmony with the self, the community, nature and the universe exists. In the centre we find reality, the Great Spirit, the Creator, God.

John Main wrote this about the centre: "The Centre is the aim of our meditation. It is the centre of our being. In the words of John of the Cross, 'God is the centre of the soul.' When our access to this centre is opened up, the Kingdom of God is established in our hearts...."

The Prayer Wheel

Laurence Freeman once said: "Prayer can be compared to an old-fashioned cartwheel with each spoke being a different form of prayer. We pray in different ways at different times, and every form of prayer is valid and effective in its own way. If one form is no longer useful in your journey to God, you replace it, like a spoke, with another form. All the spokes, like all forms of Christian prayer, must converge in the centre if the wheel is to be effective. At the centre of the wheel, we find stillness; at the centre of our soul, in this stillness, we find Christ. What makes all these forms of prayer Christian is the fact that they are centred in Christ. There can be different spokes for different folks." To quote John Main again in *The Heart of Creation,* "What you will learn from your own experience is that there is only one centre, which is in all centres."

The Still Point at the Centre

While writing this, I am ever conscious of these words of Teilhard de Chardin: "We are not human beings on a spiritual path, we are spiritual beings on a human path." I continue on my way of pilgrimage, walking the path of Christian Meditation and native spirituality into a cloud of unknowing, seeking a God who has already found me. Christian Meditation and native spirituality are not parallel paths but are actually two of the spokes which Laurence Freeman describes. They lead to the centre of all centres. Without the still point at this centre, the wheel cannot turn. And the way to the centre is through the recitation of the mantra "Maranatha" twice daily.

Pat Kasmarik

Pat Kasmarik, who lives in Valley Stream, New York, USA, was a university professor of nursing and most recently a nursing administrator. She has a doctorate in nursing and two Master's degrees in pastoral ministry and theology. She started a Christian Meditation group in Fresno, California, in 1988. In 1995 Pat joined (on a temporary basis) the Monastery of Christ the King community in London, England, and became involved in retreat and spiritual direction work.

I learned and practised Transcendental Meditation (TM) in the mid-1970s; in 1980 I was introduced to centering prayer by my pastor in Fresno. At that time the priests of the diocese were learning centering prayer as part of priestly renewal. Centering prayer replaced TM for me as a twice-daily practice. Five years later, while I was studying theology, a friend learned that my spiritual director led Christian Meditation groups in the John Main tradition. My friend, in her enthusiasm, lent me her complete collection of John Main's books.

I was struck by the similarity between the two practices. The difference I found was the emphasis in the John Main tradition on the continuous repetition of the mantra throughout the meditation. At first I was reluctant to change my practice. Then I was invited to join my spiritual director and a small group on their yearly one-week "pilgrimage" to the Montreal Priory. I stayed for three extra days as I had been ill during most of the week. It proved to be a memorable experience: the silent prayerful oneness of this large group at meditation three to five times daily. I was drawn to the Benedictine balance of prayer and work, and returned to the priory for six weeks in early 1988 and again for a week that summer.

"Be Still and Know that I Am God"

The question to be answered is this: "Why did this form of meditation take root in me so quickly and how has it been sustained?" My work was as a university professor of nursing and a Registered Nurse hospice volunteer. I was immersed intellectually and physically throughout the day; a prayer form in which I could be quiet was most inviting. The words "be still and know that I am God" have become a motto for me.

From the beginning there has been a peaceful assurance that I can "come and rest awhile" twice a day. It helps me to remain centred and present to myself, those whom I meet and those to whom I minister. As a prayer form Christian Meditation offers something different: emptying of self. We do not go to meditation in order to petition, to praise, to repent. We go to be emptied so that we might be filled with God's love. As we grow in this practice the fruits of our labours can best be seen in a growing gentleness and love of others. For me this appears in my ability to listen and be present to those whom I've cared for as a nurse or spiritual director.

Individually and collectively we are all unique. We are all God's gift and so are Christian Meditation groups. The evolution of the Fresno, California, meditation group is a study in contrasts. The group began after I returned from my third visit to the Montreal Priory in August 1988. During that fall meditators both new and not so new were spiritually energized by Fr. Laurence's annual Christian Meditation retreat at St. Anthony's Retreat House at Three Rivers, California. They responded eagerly to the word that a meditation group was forming in Fresno.

The Weekly Meditation Group

Within the first two months the group expanded from eight to twelve participants, with at least six to eight meditators coming weekly. They came to visit, to listen to Fr. John's tapes, to meditate and to ask questions about meditation, all in the tradition of the Montreal Priory. At times it was a challenge for me to remain identified specifically with meditation without stifling the group's enthusiasm for extra-curricular activities.

The group was heterogeneous with married, single, divorced and widowed men and women, most of whom were Roman

Catholic. With some urging by group members we began to share a meal after meditation every two to three months. The enthusiasm of the group lasted about two years, until major changes came into members' lives.

Several points strike me as I reflect on this time: Fr. John spoke often of the many times we start, stop and begin again in the practice of meditation. For some there are a few hiccups along the way. For others there is a need for socialization which is met in the short term by being with others, albeit silently. We are all gifted, have certain needs and are called in different ways.

One young Presbyterian psychologist and I, a privately vowed Catholic woman, continued to meet weekly after the first few years. Although always willing to invite others, we did not publicly advertise our meetings as they took place in my own small apartment. Therefore we attracted others through our own personal invitations, a Catholic pastor's referrals and my own spiritual directees. Eventually, a blind single mother of two teenage boys joined us. She had completed the Rite of Christian Initiation of Adults two years before.

This eclectic threesome met despite soccer games (our male meditator played), transportation difficulties (our blind member relied on the soccer player), and my work schedule (I worked 7 PM to 7 AM). We met at 4:45 on Sunday evenings. We became a meditating community while patiently waiting for and being open to welcoming others.

In December 1995 we discontinued our weekly meetings, as I had been invited by the Prior of the Monastery of Christ the King, London, England (Fr. Laurence Freeman's community), to become part of that community and possibly begin some form of women's community. I participated in the prayer life and ministries of retreat and spiritual direction and attended the longstanding meditation group led by Dom Willibrord Schlatman OSB. There was an interesting similarity between the London and Fresno groups in the long-term commitment of three members. Other people come and go but three remain as the core group.

God Writes Straight with Crooked Lines

This unwavering commitment continues for us, the three Fresno meditators. By any standard we are not considered a functioning meditation group. We do not meet on a regular basis. But as the three inveterate members, we constitute a Christian Meditation group in spirit. We are daily meditators who, through correspondence, have continued to share the joys and struggles of persevering in the discipline of daily meditation in the midst of challenging schedules.

God writes straight with crooked lines and so we remember "when two or three are gathered..." in the Spirit, "there I am in the midst of them."

James Logan

James Logan was born in "Hell's Kitchen," New York City, in 1949. His elementary and high school education was there, followed by four years at the University of Hawaii majoring in drama and theatre. Following a short career as a "starving actor" he joined an Eastern monastery and spent seven years in service to a guru and the practice of meditation. He is now a professional masseur at the Cornerstone Center, Phoenix, Arizona, and is South West (USA) Christian Meditation Coordinator.

It all began with a dream of the Buddha. It was a sweet, simple dream, and Buddha smiled at me. I was conveniently staying at the Pecos Benedictine Abbey in New Mexico at the time, and felt I should ask my spiritual director the next day what this dream could be about. Fr. Bob was quiet for a moment and then he fired out a name I had never heard before: "Bede Griffiths." Fr. Griffiths mentions in one of his books that "the most important spiritual guide in the church today is Fr. John Main." With the Christian Meditation seeds already planted in the deserts of Arizona, I found a meditation group to attend when I returned back home to Phoenix.

The Lost Generation of Searchers

I come from that generation of lost, searching types in the early 1970s. Leaving home four days after I finished high school, I landed in Hawaii. There I was, a theatre major at the university, trying to figure out my own character and minoring in many things that got me into trouble. My first life crisis came when the United States Army wanted to drastically change my ego. That is a long story but in short I needed God in a bad way. In the islands I lost touch with my New York Irish-Catholic background and found a disenfranchised spiritual teacher who claimed to be Yogananda's right-hand man. (Yogananda was the first Indian guru to travel to the West.) I learned Buddhist chanting and Hindu meditation and tried to fast my way into heaven.

Later I met another guru who had a big franchise and welcomed me to move in and give him my life. There was not much to give at that time, so I moved into one of his ashrams. The meditation practitioners who travelled with him were of great virtue, coming from the ancient ashram traditions of the Himalayas. The stories of masters and devotees, the wisdom of the Gita and the Upanishhads all touched a place in my soul that the church on Merric Avenue, back home, had never heard of or at least had never revealed to us.

But I lost it all. Talk about missing a few meditations: I wanted both God and the pleasures of the world in excess. The eternal boy wanted to have his cake and eat it, too. The good Lord then sent to me my next teacher, Bill Wilson, co-founder of Alcoholics Anonymous. My fall from grace opened up to me my poverty of spirit and I finally recognized God's "amazing grace."

Being one who needs the self rooted in the reality of the human consciousness of Christ, I was blessed to come across Fr. John Main. I'm back to my Catholic religion now with the contemplative heritage that jumps out of the words of scripture as my spiritual anchor.

A Beginner All Over Again

So today I am a beginner again. My computer thesaurus defines the word beginner as someone "coming into being." That's what meditation is all about: *being*. My wife has no doubt that I am a beginner, for just the other night she had to come in and rescue me when I was meditating. The space heater I was using caught fire and an electrical spark shot out from the wall. I came to screaming, knocked over the candle and spilled hot wax on myself. I fell from my chair saying something that was definitely not the mantra. She thought for sure my shadow side had finally materialized and that the true and false self were battling it out to the bitter end. There are better moments in my life, thank God, and lots of them.

John Main's guidance and the power of community were driven home to me by Paul Harris' book *John Main by Those Who Knew Him*. Books of this kind, as well as tapes and seminars, keep the flow of inspiration going so I can focus simply and with greater fidelity on the inward living mantra. It was delightful to learn in this book that Fr. Main loved the theatre. So for you, Dom John Main, the words of Shakespeare best recreate my love for your teaching: "Wonderful, wonderful, yes, wonderful and yet again wonderful, wonderful, and once more wonderful!"

William Mishler

William Mishler was born in 1940, is married and has four children and one grandson. He graduated from Holy Cross College in 1962, spent a three-year Fulbright teaching assistantship in France, and completed a Ph.D in Scandinavian studies at the University of Minnesota. He currently holds the position of Associate Professor in the Department of German, Scandinavian and Dutch at the University of Minnesota and recently has been a visiting professor at John Carroll University in Cleveland, Ohio.

In college I majored in French, and so it came about that three months after graduating, I found myself waking up one Sunday morning in a small hotel in the Latin Quarter of Paris, not far from Notre Dame Cathedral. All the church bells in the neighbourhood were ringing. Glancing at my watch I saw that it was almost nine o'clock, and throwing on my clothes I raced to Mass in Notre Dame.

Upon entering that huge stone cavern, I found Mass had just begun. The Mass was in Latin (pre-Vatican II), so in that sense not new to me, but the intonation was just strange enough, combined with the echoing magnitude of the place and the dank whiff of old stone, that suddenly I became overwhelmed with the sheer *oddness* of the experience. It was as if I had just landed from the moon. The large wave of my Catholic upbringing and Jesuit education had carried me this far and then lost all its momentum. Here I was on a strange beach. "This is not really me standing here," I said to myself, meaning that it wasn't really my conscious choice that had brought me to church that September morning, but a large array of habits, fears, and no doubt even superstitions. And so I left my seat and exited the church.

The Persistent Emptiness Within

For a good number of years after that I didn't return, other than occasionally when I was hit by a sudden nostalgia or the hope of hearing the magical words that would address the small but persistent emptiness that I now carried around inside me. And then, like countless others during the 1960s, I turned to the East to yoga, to various schools of Buddhism and, fortunately, eventually to Zen.

Not far from where I was living in Minneapolis a Zen meditation centre had recently been created, headed by a no-nonsense Japanese monk by the name of Katagiri Roshi. With Katagiri, despite his wonderful laugh and gentle manner, there was no kidding around. Looking at him, listening to him, I began to get a sense of what it might mean to pay serious attention to the spiritual component of existence.

To sit and meditate with him was very productive yet frustrating. Although you had no idea of what was going on inside of him, you could feel as palpably as frost on a December windowpane that he was facing directly into the *mystery*. He also let you know, over and over again, that rationalizing about that mystery was utterly pointless, that encountering it through meditation was *everything*.

"When the Student Is Ready"

This was a great grace for me. It cut through all the reasons I endlessly recited for not trying to get in touch with the ground of my being. The eventual effect of that grace was to turn the small, hard, negative emptiness inside me into a great hungry emptiness, so to speak. In time, when I ran across John Main's teaching "When the student is ready...", I was ready. One might wonder why I just didn't stick with Zen. The answer is that in the end it was too stark for me, too reserved. The more I meditated and the more faithfully I meditated in the Christian tradition, the more obvious it became to me that grace was abundantly flowing into my life, and that the source of that grace was Christ. It was a matter of "taste and see."

Isobel Page

Sr. Isobel Page is a Religious of the Sacred Heart, a retired teacher who spent some 40 years in classrooms across Canada. She considers herself a "survivor," as she has lived through two world wars, including the two explosions in Halifax, Nova Scotia, in 1917 and 1945. In retirement she has been involved in leading Christian Meditation groups in Ottawa and in Halifax. In the 1980s she assisted Sr. Madeleine Simon in setting up the first Christian Meditation Centre at 29 Campden Hill Rd., in London, England.

I was born into a devout Catholic family where prayer was as taken for granted as mealtime and was educated in a convent school where every action was preceded and concluded by a prayer, from the awakening bell to lights out. It was hardly strange, then, that prayer had become such a part of my existence that its influence continued through the many enticing distractions of university life and formed the foundation of my religious vocation.

From the time one enters religious life, prayer and the development of a relationship with God in Christ are the focus of each day, though every person has a unique call and a different experience. Many schools of prayer methodology exist; in my congregation, the Society of the Sacred Heart, St. Ignatius was our teacher and the Spiritual Exercises our guide, along with the wisdom of St. Madeleine Sophie, our foundress.

Times of silent prayer were part of the daily schedule, beginning with an hour in the early morning when our discursive meditation was Ignatian. This prayer had a gospel passage as background for a composition of place, three points on which to reflect and a colloquy at the close. At noon, 15 minutes had to be found for an examination of conscience with a format from the Spiritual Exercises. In the afternoon, when teaching periods were over, one had to fit in a half hour before the Blessed Sacrament. It was called Adoration and was an oasis in a very busy day, a blessed time to rest in the Lord, awake or asleep!

In addition, we sang the Little Office of Our Lady three times a day, and of course, there was daily Mass and a half-hour of communal spiritual reading. In the months of May, June and October, as well as on feast days, there was Benediction. All this added up to about five hours set aside daily for prayer.

Responsible for Our Own Prayer Life

Such a regimented life, which also included four hours or so of teaching, an hour or two of supervision and an unspecified time for preparation and correction of class work, was not an easy one, but I was happy being part of it and never dreamed of changing it. Then along came the Second Vatican Council with change in religious life as the name of the game. With the promulgation of new decrees, the rules of cloister were repealed and the wearing of a religious habit was no longer obligatory.

Religious women were encouraged to form small communities instead of living in large institutions. Such changes left individuals responsible, to a large extent, for their prayer life. If one was to remain true to her religious vocation, prayer had to continue to be the heart of her life.

The Search Is On

In the early 1970s, I happened to read the novel *Franny and Zooey* by J.D. Salinger, which piqued my interest in "The Jesus Prayer," which is an important aspect of the book. From there I was led to the mysticism of the eastern rites and read everything I could find on the subject. The Russian spiritual classic *The Way of a Pilgrim* fascinated me. Then came publications from India: Bede Griffiths, Abhishiktananda, Anthony de Mello. All had a deep effect on my approach to prayer, from breathing to yoga. Then I came across the books of William Johnston, S.J. He has remained a guru for me, but the culmination of my search was the arrival of John Main in Montreal in 1977, and the establishment of a Benedictine monastery, first at Vendome Avenue and then the Priory on Pine Avenue.

A Path for the Rest of My Life

Because of the proximity of our convent school to both these sites, our sisters made contact with the newcomers and came under the spell of Fr. John and his gift to the world. He often visited our convent and in 1979 he gave a series of talks on meditation to all the English-speaking sisters in Montreal. By then I knew that this was the path of prayer for me for the rest of my life and I was confirmed in my choice by contact with other pilgrims. In 1986–87 I had the privilege of spending a year living at the Christian Meditation Centre at Campden Hill Rd. in London, England, which was then under the direction of a religious of the Sacred Heart, Sr. Madeleine Simon.

I have never regretted the training I received in my early life from that great master of the spiritual journey, St. Ignatius, but I am full of gratitude that, in my old age, God has led me to a prayer life which, in the words of Jean Vanier, is "a secret garden made up of silence and rest and inwardness."

Jo Russell

Jo Russell is 54 and lives in Victoria, Australia, with her husband, Bill, who is newly retired from teaching. They have four grown children: Maria (30), James (29), Michael (26) and Julie-Anne (25). Jo has been an adult literacy teacher, teaching adults communication skills via the medium of teleconferencing. Her interests include gardening, music, reading, swimming, tai chi, yoga and of course meditation.

My first real introduction to meditation came in India when I visited my daughter Maria for two months in 1994–95. She had suggested we both do the annual Bodhgaya retreat in Bihar. I wondered how I'd cope with the 10 days of silence and the many sessions of sitting, walking and standing meditation each day. But Maria assured me I'd manage, and said, as an added incentive, "The vegetarian meals are amazing!" So I went and completed the 10-day retreat. I'd like to give you a taste of what I experienced there and how it set me on the path of Christian Meditation for life.

Christopher Titmuss, the leader, is a wise, generous and wonderful teacher. He is also a poet and a writer and his teachings emphasize freedom and social responsibility. The retreat was a new experience for me in so many ways. The walking meditations made me realize I'd walked "mechanically" for most of my life, without *awareness*. I learned to feel each step in this exercise. Likewise the early morning yoga sessions helped me to reconnect with my body, and through the basic asanas we practised, my posture improved. Yoga is now an essential part of my day. It took many days for me to settle down, but with the support of the whole group of over

120 meditators, the daily practice and the silence, even the simple acts of washing clothes or cleaning the toilets, were enjoyed and became a positive experience of mindfulness.

Bonding out of Silence

There were small-group sessions, work sessions, opportunities for one-to-one meetings with the teachers, talks and enquiry sessions. All these helped me to move from my initial restlessness and even rebellion towards awareness and relaxation. At first I felt isolated, but an amazing thing seems to happen when you have a group of people meditating: bonding happens not despite the silence but because of it. We were encouraged to read our body's reactions and sensations. I found I was getting to know parts of myself that I'd kept hidden. Maybe it was because I'd been in the habit for most of my life of only showing my "good" side.

Only a Few Meditators Retained Their Serenity

It wasn't all serious. Meditators need to be able to laugh at themselves. I vividly remember the time I opened my eyes during the standing meditation to see a dark shadow move towards me. I watched in horror as a rat headed for me. In fact, it ran over my foot! In the squeals and confusion that followed only a few seasoned meditators maintained their serenity.

Much wisdom was imparted in the evening talks or the enquiry sessions. We learned the benefits of leading a simple life without "attachment" so that the space this makes provides an opportunity to share and to live a life of freedom in our poverty. I learned that the practice of meditation could help me to control my desires, attitudes and feelings.

I often reread the notes I made and revisit the experience. In fact, nine months later my son James and I drove hundreds of kilometres to do a six-day retreat in a Forest Meditation Centre in Australia, again led by Christopher Titmuss. We took our own tents, ate in the open, and met for meditation and talks in the meditation hall accompanied each night either by heavy rain or a chorus of cicadas. I found I was quite relaxed in the small-group meetings, felt freer to express my feelings and could almost manage to sit cross-legged for the 45-minute meditation sessions. As in India the talks reinforced the benefits of simplifying one's life and seeking the wisdom and clarity that are needed to understand oneself, one's life and the world around us.

Meditation and Detachment

Other themes I remember are renunciation, not clinging to preconceived ideas, and realizing that we cannot always know the full truth about people or situations. However, that doesn't mean we shouldn't inquire, question, observe and reflect, both on what's going on within us and outside of us. *Detachment* is important. If we can detach ourselves from possessions we can really live in the present moment and experience the joy of being alive. In my one-to-one session with Subhana, a Zen Buddhist, she gave me a beautiful verse to help me focus on my breath. It might help others, too: As you breathe in: "I calm my mind and body." As you breathe out: "I smile, this really is a beautiful moment."

God's Language Is Silence

Two years later I attended a day on Christian Meditation led by Paul Harris in Bendigo and moved on to appreciate the importance of the mantra and how its poverty can help me come to inner stillness. I was reminded that "God's language is silence," that God speaks directly to our hearts. Afterwards, I was inspired to start a meditation group in Charlton. But first I rang the regional Catholic secondary school and offered to talk to the senior students about meditation. I was invited to take a session with 20 Year 11 students during their two-day orientation for their Year 12. Though very nervous, I was buoyed up by the thoughts and prayers and support of many friends, and keen to start the session.

Our 40-minute session included some stories of my Indian experiences and how my own practice of Christian Meditation grew out of that. I offered a guided relaxation of the whole body, a short meditation period and finally an evaluation. I was delighted with their cooperation and their willingness to try something new. I've also offered to return this year if they would like some help starting a regular meditation group.

Meanwhile, I continue to meditate each morning and most nights. It's like a wellspring for me, a source of peace, and as important to my day as eating and sleeping.

Frank Seeburger

Frank Seeburger is Professor and Chair of the Philosophy Department at the University of Denver, Colorado, USA. He has published three books as well as various articles in professional journals, including The American Benedictine Review. *In one of his classes, he takes a small group of students each spring to the Benedictine Monastery of Christ in the Desert for a few days. He lives with his wife, teenage daughter and mother in Longmont, Colorado. He is an Episcopalian.*

"Take what you are given." That was the message I encountered when I first came upon Christian Meditation in the spring of 1989. At the time, I was exactly in the right place to receive that message and the way of Christian Meditation that came with it.

By then I had already been consciously practising one form of meditation or another for two-and-a-half years. I had started out by doing no more than playing certain pieces of classical music while I lay with my eyes closed. I tried just to listen in what I thought of as a kind of musically disinterested way, as if trying to listen not so much *to* the music as *through* it. Most if not all of the time I would fail, and end up attending to the music itself, rather than to the silence from which it emerged.

As I look back on it now, I would say that this is not at all a bad way to start meditating. At the time, however, I was pretty discouraged. Nevertheless, for some reason I stuck with it.

Zen Buddhist Sitting

After I'd been listening to music that way for some months, an old friend who had once been one of my students came back into my life and taught me basic Zen Buddhist breath-counting meditation. So I took that new gift and began sitting Zen daily. In the beginning, I couldn't sit for longer than 10 minutes at a stretch. Slowly, I worked my way up to counting my breath for 30 minutes at a time. I meditated on my breathing at least once each day, sometimes more often, as the mood struck me.

For more than a year, I kept up that routine. Then a colleague and friend from my department at work suggested I investigate a slightly different Buddhist form of meditation in which one does not count as one breathes, but simply focuses on the out-breath. I took that gift, too. I began practising this new form of meditation. In that new way of meditating, however, my mind seemed to go altogether astray. My thoughts just wouldn't calm down. I seemed unanchored. Once again, however, I kept at it.

That's how things continued for the next three or four months. Then I happened to go on a weekend retreat for participants in the Twelve Step Program. After checking in, I went to sit in the lobby of the retreat house. There was a book lying on the end table next to me. I picked it up. Intrigued by the title, I began to read.

Light Within by Laurence Freeman

The book was *Light Within: The Inner Path of Meditation* by Fr. Laurence Freeman. As I had earlier taken the gifts of guidance offered to me by my two friends, so now I took the gift I found in Fr. Laurence's words. The very next morning I began saying my word, "Maranatha," as I sat on the floor of my room at the retreat centre. As the book directed, I sat again later that same day, repeating my new word, letting it provide the focus and anchor that I so badly needed in my meditation at that point. I still continue to say it, meditating regularly twice a day, as Fr. Laurence taught me to do in that first of his books I read.

The Word Led Me into the Church

The way along which that word has led me in the years since then has continued to be filled with surprises. The biggest surprise to those who knew me, but above all to myself, came when, in Advent of 1990, I was baptized a Christian. Thus, the *word* led me into the church.

It also led me to more than one Benedictine monastery for personal retreats. That included the Benedictine Priory of Montreal in the spring of 1990, before I was even baptized. There I met Fr. Laurence, and soon thereafter I enrolled as an oblate novice with the community of the Priory. I already had my non-refundable plane tickets to return to the Priory a year later, for my final oblation, before I received notice of its closing. So I followed my word to the mother-house of the Priory, using my ticket to visit Mount Saviour Monastery in New York. I also visited, and still continue to visit, the Monastery of Christ in the Desert in New Mexico, as well as that community's informal sister-house, the Abbey of St. Walburga in Boulder, Colorado, not far from where I live with my family. There, I eventually did make my final oblation.

As I continued to travel the way of Christian Meditation, a small group of others joined me. For more than four years, we met twice monthly to meditate together. We were a diverse group, and we prided ourselves on welcoming all interested newcomers of whatever faith. After four years, we ceased meeting formally as a group. But each of us still continues to practise meditation, and we keep in touch as best we can. Perhaps one day we will reconvene as a group, if that gift is once more offered to us.

The Silence Is the Same for All of Us

In the meantime I continue to meditate on my own, and sometimes in group settings where others are practising other forms of contemplative prayer, such as the "Centering Prayer" which is popular in Colorado. I am quite comfortable following my teachers, Fr. John Main and Fr. Laurence, in the midst of others following such teachers as Frs. Thomas Keating and Basil Pennington. The silence is the same for all of us, I've found. I continue to take the gift that has been given to me, the gift of the word *Maranatha* and that gift continues to *give*.

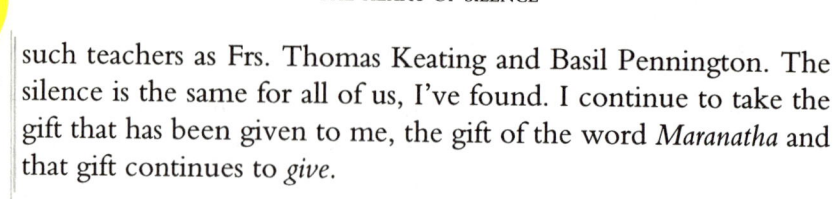

Chapter 4

On Discovering John Main

"The Teacher I Had Been Looking For"

Steve Cartwright
John Cotling
Yvonne (Main) Fitzgerald
Gregory J. Ryan
Madeleine Simon
Sheila Walshe

Steve Cartwright

Steve Cartwright, who lives in Kalamazoo, Michigan, USA, was raised in the Evangelical Brethren Church, which became the United Methodist Church in 1968. In 1972 he had a "conversion experience" while watching a Billy Graham youth rally. After officer training and service with the US Army, he earned a Master of Divinity degree and served in different United Methodist parishes. He is currently a doctoral candidate in medieval history at Western Michigan University. He leads a meditation group in Kalamazoo and is regional coordinator of Christian Meditation groups in Michigan, Illinois, Indiana and Ohio.

I grew up in a fairly typical mainline Protestant church, in which I learned, by teaching and example, that prayer was "talking to God." I accepted that and as a child prayed in this way, making a child's self-centred requests, asking God for things that I wanted. This continued through my adolescence, even after my initial conversion experience at the age of 15 while watching a Billy Graham youth crusade on television.

It was during my undergraduate years at the University of Michigan that, while studying religion and history, I became acquainted with the larger Christian tradition of prayer and spirituality. *The Imitation of Christ* by Thomas à Kempis taught me about loving God for himself, apart from anything he might give me. Thomas Kelly's *Testament of Devotion* taught me about the perpetual presence of God. I also read books about Christian Zen, and experimented briefly and unsuccessfully with things such as staring at a point on the wall. I had no one to teach me anything about prayer and spiritual discipline. The evangelical Protestant teachings I was also following at that time discouraged anything "Eastern," so I dropped such things, and continued to try to "talk to God."

Sacred Space and the Inner Experience

After college, I spent three years in the Army, mostly in Germany, where I indulged my love of history in travels to places of interest, specifically ancient churches. I came to love the experience of walking into a medieval church and sensing the presence of God amidst the arches and stained-glass windows. I realized how important sacred space was for leading me to a desire for a deeper inner experience of God.

After the Army I entered the seminary to prepare for pastoral ministry, to which I had felt called as a teenager. Though I hungered for a deeper experience of God and a more satisfying prayer life, I was not able to find what I was looking for spiritually at the seminary. Most seminarians don't. By now I was growing weary of trying to talk to God; prayer in that fashion meant little to me.

When I did pray, it was fruitless. I was realizing the futility of spending time thinking up things to say to God, such as how great he was, how much help I needed, how sorry I was for my sins, and on and on. I knew there was more to prayer than this. I did know about the existence of Christian mysticism and I had felt the presence of God in my life a number of times. I just didn't know where to go or what to do. This spiritual confusion combined with personal disappointment began to create great doubt in my life.

The Mother Church of World Methodism

Fortunately, in 1984, after my second year in the seminary, I went to England to spend a year as the assistant pastor of Wesley's Chapel in London, "the Mother Church of World Methodism." I became a member of the Wesley Community, a small live-in Christian community that shared prayers and meals. There I again found sacred space where, in weekly worship, I sensed the presence of God in the awe-inspiring acoustics and ambience of the Chapel. It was there that I first learned of meditation, from Roy Kilner, a British Methodist prison chaplain who preached occasionally at the Chapel and taught meditation from the pulpit.

My Introduction to John Main

Though I was sceptical at first, because I still believed personal prayer ought to have some kind of discursive content, I began to realize that perhaps meditation was the way of prayer I had been looking for. One of the Wesley Community members was also exploring meditation and had met with Sr. Madeleine Simon, and spoke of John Main's teaching on meditation. It took time and more travels in Britain, again to more sacred places, to convince me to look into meditation. I felt the presence of God very strongly at Fountains Abbey, and again in the Orkney Islands. These experiences restored my faith. A month or so before I left England, in July 1985, I visited Sr. Madeleine at the Christian Meditation Centre in London, talked with her, and bought copies of John Main's *Word into Silence* and *The Gethsemani Talks*. It only took one reading to convince me that I had found what I was looking for.

A Small, Struggling, but Committed Group

I brought the practice of meditation back to the States with me and I persisted in its daily discipline, sharing it with those parishioners I thought would be open to it. I contacted the Benedictine Priory in Montreal and, during my years of pastoral ministry, made three trips there. When I came to Kalamazoo in 1990 to study medieval history, I saw a poster advertising meditation at St. Thomas More Student Parish, and contacted Mary Ann Kundtz, the leader of the courses. We established an immediate friendship and spiritual bond, and over the next four years cooperated in leading meditation classes and establishing a meditation group. Mary Ann has since moved to Colorado, leaving me and Bruce Martin to lead the group here. We are a small, struggling group, but we are committed to the inner experience of meditation. We have learned humility and the importance of poverty; we have also learned to abandon expectations and to begin anew each week.

Today I meditate as faithfully as I can (sometimes with my dog and cat!). I also study the tradition of Christian Meditation, to make clear to others its deep Christian roots. At Fr. Laurence's urging, I hope eventually to compile a collection of ancient and medieval testimonies to meditation, in order to help meditators understand the tradition better. I combine the academic study of meditation's history with my own practice, and I find this deepens my own experience of this way of contemplative prayer.

John Cotling

John Cotling is a retired textile-firm manager in Manchester, England. He founded one of the first Christian Meditation groups in England in 1977, is coordinator of meditation in the northwest area of England and, for 18 years, has been active in the St. Vincent de Paul Society. Four years ago he started a Christian Meditation Centre based in his own home.

I first came into contact with meditation through a school of philosophy. But because its tradition had a Hindu base, I did not feel comfortable and subsequently gave it up. Then, one Sunday while I was reading one of the Catholic papers, I saw an advertisement for three introductory tapes on Christian Meditation. This was new to me. I sent for the tapes, which were talks by Fr. John Main.

My three tapes arrived and I played them over and over again. I listened to them with a critical mind but I could not fault them. At last I knew in my heart that I had found a real teacher of prayer. To find that kind of teacher in our busy materialistic society is a great blessing. Even now, after 20 years, John Main's talks still inspire me with the freshness and the authenticity that struck me the first time I heard them. To me they are a tremendous legacy for future generations. Fr. John teaches with the courage and conviction of one who was commissioned by the Spirit to share with those of like mind and heart and to pass on a way of prayer, the path of meditation.

The Teacher and the Practice

To me Fr. John is the teacher of the twentieth century. He uses the modern tool of our times, the cassette tape; he teaches with the spoken word; and his insights and words are charged with the breath of life. Fr. John teaches also by sound. A purity of sound is a great teacher. Silence is the greatest purity of sound; we find this silence through the repetition of the mantra.

After 20 years, and in hindsight, I think it is *the practice* that is the most important thing in meditation. Only practice, as Fr. John would say, verifies the experience within you. Only the practice teaches us what faithfulness, patience and charity really mean. Of course these words only point the way; practice teaches the truth from within. The practice of meditation brings one peace, love for others and "oneness" with God.

The Fruits of the Practice

If I ask myself what external benefits meditation has brought me, I would have to say that, since my retirement from work, my life has been full of peace, joy and abundance. One of the most important gifts of treading this path of prayer has been meeting my fellow travellers on the way. They, too, have endorsed the road we travel as the right one. I have met many meditators from around the world, people whom I would never have met if it had not been for meditation. I recognize our interconnectedness, our oneness. I think I am beginning to understand that to be in communion is necessary before we can really communicate.

The Greatest Journey Is Inward

But I must return to the daily practice in order to bring life to this oneness. As Jesus said, "Let them all be one, Father, as I am in you and you in me." We now live in a world of hi-tech communication. We have Internet, satellite stations, computers; we can fly to the moon; television brings us world news; and we are still reaching out further to Mars and beyond. But I still believe that the greatest journey we can make is the journey inward to our own heart, the true centre, and there find the truth of our own being. At that centre we are one with the creative energy of the universe; we are at one with the one who is. The beginning and the end of all communication is communion that leads to *oneness*.

Yvonne (Main) Fitzgerald

Yvonne Fitzgerald, sister to John Main, lives in Booterstown, Dublin, Ireland, and was recently widowed for the second time. She has two children. Since her brother's death she has played a leading role in bringing John Main's teaching to Ireland, where there are now 100 Christian Meditation groups. (Note: John Main's given name was Douglas, so Yvonne uses it here. John was a name given in his Benedictine religious community.)

Many people ask me about the early life of my brother Douglas (John Main). We were a happy Irish family of six children growing up in London, England. We did the usual things, such as birthday parties and holidays to the seaside, and eventually settled in a house in Sussex. That house was a great joy for many years. One of our favourite activities as children was drama. Douglas was very good at producing plays. We had an Irish maid and once as we were practising for a play she decided to introduce us to our Irish heritage by teaching us some IRA songs. When Mother discovered our newfound ability at singing Irish songs, she was horrified.

A few times, as a young child, Douglas would celebrate Mass with an altar on top of a chest of drawers. I was encouraged to be an altar girl but was frequently dismissed because I either started to laugh or rang the bell at the wrong time.

John Main's Sense of Humour

Douglas had a tremendous sense of humour and he and our brother Ian were always playing practical jokes. The day of King George V's funeral, my mother and a friend were listening to the service on the radio. The commentator was saying: "Now the funeral has arrived at Euston Station and the royal family are following the hearse and the coffin." A voice then cut in: "Oh, good gracious, a terrible thing has happened, the coffin has fallen off the hearse and the king is rolling down the steps ..." My mother and her friend were duly horrified. They did not know that Ian and Douglas had rigged up another piece of radio equipment and had managed to interrupt the radio broadcast with their horrible announcement. The rest of the children were in the hallway in hysterics.

During our summer holidays the greatest joy for Douglas and me was to visit a nearby graveyard and change all the flowers around, saying, "Look at this poor fellow, he has nothing and his neighbour has far too many bouquets." Mother was delighted to have peace for such long intervals. At other times we would take neighbourhood children for walks. Their mothers thought we were such lovely children but we only wanted to have races with the prams!

World War II

When the war broke out in 1939, Douglas was 13. He and I were fire watchers. We were both issued with helmets (tin hats). As soon as an air-raid siren would sound, the two of us would put on our hats and madly dash out of doors; Mother would say, "Come back here immediately!" We were both convinced that with the protection of our tin hats absolutely nothing could possibly happen to us. At that time we did not realize the dangers of war. My memory of those days is of sleeping under the dining-room table during air raids and of someone inevitably saying, "Let's have a cup of tea!"

The story of Douglas' life and his discovery of meditation is well told in two books, *In the Stillness Dancing: The Journey of John Main* (Neil McKenty) and *John Main by Those Who Knew Him* (Paul Harris) and in a recently published booklet, *The Life and Teaching of John Main* (Paul Harris).

"Meditation Is Not for Me"

Strangely enough, I didn't begin to meditate until after the death of Douglas in 1982. He did once talk to me about meditation but I replied at the time, "I don't think that's for me." What led me eventually to meditation was coming to Montreal and the Benedictine Priory with my sister Diane for his funeral. It was one of the great emotional experiences of my lifetime. Diane and I were totally overcome by the goodness and kindness of everyone at the

Priory and amazed at the outpouring of love and affection for Douglas. It took me a year to internalize Douglas' death and at the end of the year I returned to the Priory in Montreal and there began to realize that meditation was indeed to be my spiritual path.

The Transformation from Within

Back in Ireland I joined a meditation group at Holy Angels Convent. Then some months later Laurence Freeman came to Dublin and suggested I start a group at my own home in Sandymount. Over the years I have come to see the self-authenticating aspects of meditation and the goodness and compassion that flow from this daily spiritual discipline. I can see what it has done for others and I realize the transformation within myself.

Not an Easy Path

My second husband, who died a year ago, was an alcoholic. Sometimes life could be very trying. Meditation helped me to get through the dark times. Not that meditation is an easy path – as every meditator can acknowledge, it is often a most difficult path. Fr. Pat Murray, who was a friend of Douglas', just last week pointed out that he finds meditation more and more difficult as he travels along the path of this way of prayer. My prayer life was very naked before discovering meditation. Now a new world has opened up the scriptures for me and it's great to be awake.

No Expectations, No Goals, No Objectives

Douglas, in his teaching, is always saying we should come to meditation with no expectations, no goals and no objectives. We are not trying to accomplish anything, just *be*. But this is hard to understand because in our society we are constantly conditioned to *achieve* something through our human efforts. Recently an 80-year-old man asked me, "What are you trying to achieve in meditation?" I replied, "We are not really trying to achieve anything. There is no goal, just a time for *being*, being in the presence of Christ." He could not understand this at all. "But surely," he said, "there must be a goal. You must be aiming at achieving something." I simply couldn't make him see the point. Perhaps the more cerebral one is, the more difficult it is to grasp this truth.

Meditation Creates Community

After my husband's death I went through a very lonely time. I had never lived alone in my life and found it so strange and such an eerie feeling not to have anyone to whom to say "good morning" or "good night." I began to realize then that I am really a *community person*. I am now involved in several projects which involve others in the meditating community.

This past summer my nephew William Main and I leased a summer convent from the Presentation sisters in Ballinskelligs, County Kerry, where Douglas spent part of his youth. In May meditators came from near and far to enjoy a summer holiday with three daily times of meditation.

And recently I became involved in bringing Sister Ishpriya, a Sacred Heart Sister from India, to conduct the annual Dublin School of Prayer. She is a Christian presence among Hindu sangases in India, and will explore the insights and practices of Eastern spiritual traditions. Douglas will be smiling at this as he learned to meditate from a Hindu swami.

Gregory J. Ryan

Gregory J. Ryan lives in Wall, New Jersey, USA, is married with two grown children and is a Benedictine oblate. He is editor of The Burning Heart: Reading the New Testament with John Main *and author of* Meditation, Plain and Simple *and* My Happy Heart, Meditation for Children; *he has published articles on Thomas Merton and modern monasticism in* Cistercian Studies Quarterly, Monastic Studies, Sisters Today, *and* The Merton Seasonal. *He is the regional coordinator, WCCM/USA Communications Coordinator and web-custodian for www.wccm.org. He teaches second grade in a local school.*

In September 1970, fresh out of college, I began my teaching career with the Selective Service System nipping at my heels. With the Vietnam War still being waged, the draft had gone to a lottery system and my number (215) was a "winner." It remains the only lottery I have ever won!

By Thanksgiving I was a newlywed, and by Eastertime I was a civilian conscientious objector (C.O.) working as an attendant in the psychiatric ward of a New Jersey state hospital. The people there were quite an interesting mixture, making it difficult sometimes to determine who was the patient and who was the worker. Myself included! A fellow C.O. working on the ward passed along a couple of books written by Thomas Merton. I was immediately captivated by them and I have been reading him ever since.

Merton's dedication to a life of prayer was perhaps not everyone's image of what a life of prayer might be, but this struck me as a necessary element in anyone's life. The only trouble was he did not set out a "program" of prayer for a person in my situation. Everything seemed rather vague. Regular Mass attendance seemed to me an important yet only a partial participation in the divine life, but adding more "devotions" did not seem any better.

Contemplative Prayer from the Pulpit

It wasn't until 1976, when a newly-assigned Irish-born parish priest used the words "contemplative prayer" from the pulpit, that I was prompted to speak to him of all that I had been reading in Merton. His answer was not to be "afraid" of prayer, a curious choice of words, I thought. He also invited me to meet with him each Friday night for a couple of hours of prayer, a practice that he had followed in his previous parishes. And so the two of us, along with an occasional newcomer, met each Friday evening from 7 to 9 PM. We would take turns selecting a reading from a classic book on prayer, such as *The Cloud of Unknowing*, or New Testament readings, and then we spent an hour in silent prayer. It was very peaceful, but it was a bit "complicated."

The Teaching I Had Been Looking For

I sent out inquiries to several Cistercian monks about how to go about setting up a contemplative prayer group. They were generous with suggestions but they were also a bit complicated, with the exception of the response from Brother Patrick Hart, Merton's secretary at the Abbey of Gethsemani. Brother Pat sent me transcriptions of several conferences Fr. John Main had given to the community at Gethsemani in 1976 before moving from his monastery in London to found the community in Montreal. These were first published serially in *Cistercian Studies* and later in book form as *Christian Meditation: The Gethsemani Talks*. I immediately recognized that this was the teaching I had been looking for.

Getting a Group Started

Another monk, Brother Francis of St. Joseph's Abbey in Spencer, Massachusetts, later lent me a set of audiotapes of Fr. John giving his introductory sessions on Christian Meditation. This was all I needed to hear. I contacted Fr. John and in 1980, on the Feast of Saint Laurence, I became an oblate member of the Benedictine Priory of Montreal. A few months later, Fr. Laurence came to New Jersey and gave an introductory session, which helped get our weekly meditation group started. We have been meeting in various locations ever since. While we started with only Catholics in the group, we have grown to include members of various religious backgrounds and traditions.

A Life Rooted in Prayer

During my two brief visits to the monastery Fr. John was very accessible and easy to talk to. He was simple and direct as he encouraged me on the pilgrimage of meditation. He taught me that there is no way of prayer that can be *added* to my life, but that my life is already *rooted in prayer*, the Spirit of God living in all of us. Meditation is a daily practice whereby we set aside all distractions of the day simply to be open to that reality. I saw this as the teaching of the gospel: dying to self only to find life. Merton's writings had pointed me in this direction, but Fr. John showed me the way.

Our family visited the monastery several times after Fr. John's death. When they were ready, our daughters Caitlin and Abigail each made their first communion there with Fr. Laurence guiding them along. My wife, Liz, became an oblate-novice, but the monastery closed before her final oblation.

A Blessing for Everyone

While, at the time, the closing of the Montreal monastery was a sad event for us, in hindsight it has been a blessing for everyone. It reminds me of the Zen koan: "Where do you go from the top of a 30-foot pole?" Where does a community go once its monastery has closed? The answer: *Everywhere!* The World Community for Christian Meditation continues the work begun by Fr. John and Fr. Laurence those many years ago, first in London and then in Montreal. The meditation centres, groups and individual meditators around the world witness to the universality of the life of the Spirit living in our hearts.

Openness to the Working of the Spirit

When I first went to Montreal I rather short-sightedly saw it as a sort of closure; it seemed to be the end of a long journey that had started with the first book I had read by Thomas Merton. Fr. John must have sensed this. During the Mass in which I made my oblation, he commented that since the time I had first contacted him, no one could have foreseen the relationship that had developed between us. But more importantly, he wondered, who could predict the direction in which it would go from that moment on? That openness to the working of the Spirit is what I reckon to be the hallmark of Fr. John's life and teaching: a deep-seated faith in the abiding presence of God no matter what. The daily practice of meditation makes me sensitive to that presence and challenges me to seek it in all facets of my life.

Madeleine Simon

Sister Madeleine Simon, 88 years old, is a religious of the Sacred Heart in London, England. She founded the Christian Meditation Centre in London in 1986 and a second centre in Royston near Cambridge in 1988. She first met John Main in 1963; they remained lifelong friends. She is the author of Born Contemplative, *a book on how to introduce children to Christian Meditation, and has played a pivotal role in introducing John Main's teaching in the United Kingdom.*

Have you ever hugged a tree? I have. Young arms meeting round young oak, cheek rubbing against young bark. Fifty years later, returning to my old school, I found that tree again, stately, mature, but just as lovable. No, I am not crazy but I had very good reason for caressing it. I found God so lovable I had to have a way of caressing him. I just knew, somehow, that God was totally present in that tree as in every other tree, flower and blade of grass. I was hugging him present there. We were both present to the tree and therefore to each other. So my reasoning went at the age of about 13, and I have never had cause to alter it. My odyssey had begun.

Another memory that belongs to school days was my delight at discovering a wonderful sentence as I was ploughing my way through an interminable prayer in a prayer book I had been given called *Flowers of Nazareth*. "As pants the hart for living streams, so longs my soul for Thee, O Lord," I read. This just expressed my own longing for God. Next time round I skipped the first couple of pages of the prayer so as to get to this passage more quickly, and after a bit I opened the book at the place where it was and stayed there, feeling guilty about all the unread pages before and after.

I Felt I Had Really Come Home

My contemplative bent has never left me. In due course I entered with the nuns with whom I had been at school and was allowed to follow my contemplative way of prayer. But it was many years later, when I came to know Dom John Main and heard about the mantra, that I felt I had really come home. What to do about distractions had always been a worry for me and now everything fell into place. With every distraction I just turned back to the mantra and so to the silent presence of God. Ten distractions meant ten willed returns to the Presence, and this, I realized, was a way of pure prayer.

I first met Fr. John in 1963 when he came to give our community a three-day retreat. He based his talks on the church and, though the community in general was very impressed by what he had to say, I have to confess that the talks left me cold. He asked to see me because my father André, who knew some cousins of his, had been to visit him when he was studying at San Anselmo and he had been very touched that an elderly man like my father should have taken the trouble to call on him. I remember him as genial and friendly during this visit but I was not left with any particular desire to meet him again – nor did I for another 12 years.

"I Stomped in, Boots and All"

In 1975 our Sister Sara Grant, from the Christa Prema Seva Ashram in Poona, was in England. We met in Southall, a strongly Indian township west of London where I was living, to discuss a possible ashram-type prayer centre there in which Sikhs, Hindus and Moslems might feel free enough to pray in silence with us. Sr. Sara asked me to drive her to an address in Ealing where I intended to drop her and return home.

However, the tall, black-habited figure on the doorstep, none other than Fr. John, invited me in and I found myself in my clumping winter boots in a room full of silent people. Fr. John asked Sr. Sara to speak and we then all moved to another room for meditation. I was feeling so nervous that I stomped in, boots and all. After the meditation we went back to the original room where questions were put to Sr. Sara about her ashram. By the time I left I was saying to myself: "This is for me." Fr. John had scarcely spoken except to introduce his guest. From that time I was a regular attendee at the meditation meetings.

"We Had Met at a Deep Level"

One evening, after the group had returned from the meditation room, Fr. John turned and asked me a question directly. As I answered, we both knew that we had met at a deep level. Nothing was ever said about this by either of us until the last talk I had with him in Montreal in May 1982, and he said something to this effect: "Our love for each other, and indeed for everyone else, is one with God's love."

His guidance, at least in my case, was non-directive; he answered my questions and he recommended books. Once I asked him what he considered to be the essential teaching of meditation. Without hesitation he answered, "Love." He did not expound, but my understanding of that answer has been deepening ever since. During a six-week renewal period he gave me *Saccidananda* to ponder, and for the only other retreat I made under his guidance, he gave me Meister Eckhart. Both of these books have had a profound influence on my spiritual development. He did not ask for, nor did I give, any account of their effect on me.

John Main and His Humour

No memoir of Fr. John could be complete without some mention of his humour and gift of mimicry which sparkled out at the most unexpected moments. Having just delivered a profound and most beautiful talk on prayer, he said he was willing to take questions. An awed silence ensued which he defused by adding with a mischievous twinkle: "So, as General de Gaulle said at his first news conference: 'Ladies and gentlemen, be so good as to provide questions for my answers.'"

During my visit to the Montreal community in the spring of 1982, it seemed to me that Fr. John's spirituality had come to the simplicity of St. John's "God is love." I remember him saying: "God is a sea of love; rest in that love, act out of that love. If you have had a difficulty with others, remember that river of love within you and begin to pour out love on them again."

God Is Like a Blazing Fire

At the Holy Saturday vigil there was a blazing fire in the hall which lit us all up in its glow. Fr. John, as celebrant, was standing apart near the fire. Looking into it, he said that God is like a blazing fire of love, and that we need to throw ourselves into it, to be one with it, and then to take that fire which is the love of God out into our lives that others may burn with it too.

In the summer of 1982 I saw him in London. I noticed a slight awkwardness in his walk, and a friend in Ireland told me how once he winced when getting out of her small car, but none of us knew of his advanced cancer or foresaw that in six months his pilgrimage would be over. I spoke to him on the phone just before he left for the airport and his last journey back to Canada. As I put the phone down I experienced a wonderful sense of peace, serenity and holiness. That is how I know him still.

A Time of Final Maturing

Now, nearly two decades later, I have reached old age, and happily I still have my faculties. I am aware that all these years of meditation have helped to prepare me for this time of final maturing. They have given me a certain freedom which enables me to accept the slowing-down process and the inevitable disabilities of this time of life. The norm for times of meditation remains twice daily, but I have to accept that this must be adapted or even omitted on occasion.

A growing dependence on others is a *sine qua non* of old age whether one is in dementia or still alert. It can be a struggle to accept this dependence and diminution, as memory becomes less reliable and concentration more difficult to sustain. But as time goes on, the aged often come to a freedom which brings in its wake a quiet love and a kinship with all. There is a gracious awareness that perfect fulfilment lies in perfect surrender to the loss of everything.

"Unless You Become Like Little Children"

It is unfortunate that the term "second childhood" is only used in a negative sense. For those with dementia the use of the negative is easier to understand, but even then, with the loss of responsibility for one's actions, there comes a certain return to the age of innocence. I have quoted to myself the hymn title "This Is Holy Ground" as I watch the silent little procession of caregivers bringing the mentally sick along to the dining room.

Our meditation, practised over the years, will have helped us to live in the present moment. May it now lead us towards that final maturity of "second childhood" which Jesus was speaking about when he said, *"I assure you that unless you change and become like children, you will never enter the Kingdom of Heaven."*(Matthew 18:3)

Sheila Walshe

Sheila Walshe lives in Dalkey, County Dublin, Ireland, and is the administrator of Monsignor Tom Fehily's Christian Meditation Centre in Dun Laoghaire, County Dublin. She was a member of an organizational team for the 1997 John Main Seminar held in Dublin which featured a meditator, the new President of Ireland, Mary McAleese, as the guest seminar speaker.

I was born in the third decade of the twentieth century, and from my earliest childhood I was attracted to silent prayer. One of my hallowed memories is of a place in County Clare, Ireland, called Cratloe. Here, at the top of a hill, the villagers had erected with their own hands a grotto of Our Lady of Lourdes. And still higher up, overlooking the grotto, was Calvary.

On summer evenings I loved to climb up, alone, to the grotto and remain for some time there in silent prayer. More and more I grew to love silence as the seed-bed in which prayer thrives. My first two spiritual directors were Jesuits, and then for the next 40 years I was directed by two Carmelite fathers. For years my spiritual nourishment came from the works of St. John of the Cross, as I read and reread each of his four volumes.

As mentioned, like many of my generation, I was brought up by Jesuits in the Exercises of St. Ignatius, which at that time focused on discursive prayer. I am grateful for that experience, but very early on I felt drawn towards a deeper prayer, and for many years I practised the Prayer of Recollection. This practice of the presence of God was my life force.

God Is Never Outdone in Generosity

In later years, a certain spiritual restlessness seemed to overtake me. One day in 1989 I was invited to a talk by Paul Harris in Dublin on Christian Meditation as taught by John Main. This talk proved to be a turning point in my prayer life and spiritual journey. After the talk I left convinced that this was what I had been looking for all my life.

I needed John Main's discipline and his requirement for a person to meditate morning and evening, every day. This completely God-centred prayer has been a great gift. It has anchored and grounded me. Little things which previously might have upset me I now seem to take in my stride. I am very conscious of God's presence and direction in my life. His help is there even in little things. He is never outdone in generosity. I seem freer, and this freedom allows God to act through me. I know that any good is not coming from me but from God.

Reciting the Mantra at Other Times

I have a few hints that have helped me on the path of meditation. First, I make sure my morning meditation is always early, first thing in the day upon waking. Second, I find it helpful at various moments during the day to repeat the mantra. This can be done while standing in a supermarket line, waiting in a car, washing dishes or riding on a bus. This helps to root the mantra deep in one's heart. The mantra can even be a great friend in a dentist's chair, before surgery, or whenever we face anxiety, crisis or trauma in our life.

My late Dublin friend and meditator Lucy McDonald once said, "It seems to me that the mantra is the most revolutionary spiritual teaching in the world today." I would like to echo Lucy's sentiments. It has transformed and changed my life and set me on a joyous spiritual path.

Chapter 5

Meditation and Married Life

"It Has Deepened Our Relationship"

Robbie Bishop
Tom Cain
Maurie Costello
Patricia Gulick
Leon Milroy
Marlene Sweeney
Judi Taylor

Robbie Bishop

Robbie Bishop lives at Bouncers Farm, Essex, in England, and is married to Olga. They have five children. Robbie and Olga lived and worked for many years in Italy but are now retired; they began meditating seven years ago. They recently participated in a Christian Meditation pilgrimage to the Holy Land.

My story goes back a number of years. For a long time, my sister Maureen had been trying to persuade Olga to meditate in an Eastern tradition. As a result, Olga had gone up to London a few times to try it out but had not continued. I myself felt that Indian-style meditation was not my sort of thing at all: much too exotic and trendy for me.

Eventually, in January 1992, Maureen heard that there was to be a weekend introduction to Christian Meditation, which she thought might appeal to both of us. The weekend was to take place at New Hall, which is only four or five miles from our house. New Hall was at one time one of Henry VIII's great manors. It is now a Catholic school and retreat house. My sisters and daughters had gone to school there, and Olga and I had been to New Hall on a number of other occasions. It was close by so we decided to go.

The weekend started on Friday evening, in order to enable people to congregate in good time for the serious beginning of proceedings next day. As we lived so close to New Hall, Olga and I decided to go only on Saturday morning.

When we came into the meeting-room, my heart sank. There were a number of people who, perhaps because they had met the night before, all seemed to know each other. A group congregated round the person whom I identified as the speaker. They were talking animatedly. I was not interested in their talk. I felt excluded. I concluded that this was not for me.

However, I could not leave at that precise moment without drawing attention to myself. I told Olga I would stay only until the coffee-break and then leave inconspicuously. If she wanted to stay, I would come back and fetch her in the evening.

Meanwhile, everybody sat down and the speaker, Paul Harris, began. Within five minutes my whole attitude changed. His talk – so simple, honest and sincere – carried me quite away. I don't now remember all the points he made, but some have stuck with me. He said that "the practice of Christian Meditation was very simple, but not easy."

Say Your Mantra

"Just repeat your mantra; say it peacefully and calmly; and give your mind a rest from all the everyday worries and problems of the world that crowd in on you," he continued. "Don't worry about your progress or how you're doing," he said. "Take a leap of faith into the hands of the unknown, the hands of God."

There were, and are, many questions about the practice of meditation, such as "What effect does meditation have on the person?" "What difference does it make?" I can only speak for myself. I personally do not feel any difference, any change in me. However, other people, friends who know me well, say that I have changed. In what way have I changed? I don't know. You would have to ask my friends.

Meditation in the Christian tradition as taught by the speaker was simple, sincere, a daily discipline, and completely unflamboyant. After the meeting I said to Olga that I thought it would be good if we started meditating. So we did. I also asked her if she knew of any others in our village who might be interested. She did not. So we meditated on our own.

The Role of the Meditation Group

Some weeks later, Olga heard that there was a group in the village wanting to contact others who might wish to meditate. We joined this group. The leaders, a man and his wife, much younger than we, are Anglican Franciscan tertiaries. We meet once a week, in the evening. It is not a social occasion but a time for prayer. First we listen to one of the John Main tapes, then we meditate, and then we return home. That's all there is to our meetings. Initially, we used to meet in our own houses in succession. Now we meet in the hall attached to the parish church. The group consists of a varying number of people, to a maximum of seven. However, sometimes the number falls to two or even one.

Since those first days, in addition to meditating at home, Olga and I have been to various Christian Meditation functions, including Laurence Freeman's retreats at Montee Oliveto, conferences at Ascot and Ampleforth, the John Main Seminar with the Dalai Lama and the recent retreat pilgrimage to Israel.

Why do I continue to participate in the weekly meetings? All I can say is that the atmosphere at the meetings is unique. There is a special sense of fellowship and bonding, a sense of a united commitment, and yet no solemnity. Perhaps that "difference" which no meditators can see in themselves but which is obvious to their friends keep drawing us all back to the source of life and grace in the group setting.

Tom Cain

Tom Cain lives in Lethbridge, Alberta, Canada, and is married with a daughter (22) and a son (18). He works as an advocate for people with disabilities in southern Alberta and says that the practice of meditation has helped him to recognize their "deeper" needs and desire for relationships. He has meditated for 19 years and is regional coordinator for Christian Meditation in southern Alberta.

I would like to share some of my experiences before and after I was enticed into the practice of meditation. This is also a story of being rejected by the community while regaining a sense of community in the practice of meditation.

As a middle-aged person, I cherish fond memories of my parish work as an ordained Catholic priest. I have always been a busy person. When I left the formal clergied ministry in order to marry and raise a family, I continued to be very busy, working on behalf of people with disabilities. In 1980, I had just finished a very intense five-year period. I took that summer off and promised that I would never work that hard again. I truly started to claim one day a week as simply a "*be*-day" – a time to *be*, not do.

For Christmas that year my mother-in-law asked me to get her some tapes about prayer to listen to since her eyesight was beginning to fail her. After listening to the tapes on centering prayer, she said they asked her to be too quiet. She explained, "I have to *talk* to God." She was the first person who ever gave me back a Christmas gift and said, "Maybe these were intended for you." That was my start with Christian Meditation and I meditated faithfully *once* a day for about 20 minutes for eight years.

Going Away Gift: Moment of Christ

A friend who was leaving Lethbridge in 1988 gave me a copy of *Moment of Christ* by John Main as a going-away gift. That led me to read other books by John Main, where I found out that I could be enriched by praying *twice* a day. I was amazed, after eight years of praying by myself, that there were Christian Meditation groups all over the world. After I read *Community of Love* I called the monastery in Montreal and found out that in a few weeks there was going to be a national gathering of meditators. I decided to go. The primary thing that struck me in Montreal was the wide variety of people and age groups represented. This made meditation seem do-able, if people from all walks of life were called to this quiet experience.

After Paul Harris gave a series of talks in Lethbridge on Christian Meditation in February 1993, our local newspaper interviewed me as part of a follow-up article on meditation. My answer to a question about meditation was, "It's like going for a walk with your favourite person. You are both there and conscious of each other's presence. You are enjoying each other but you don't need to say anything."

I also told the reporter that I had formerly been active in parish work without really knowing how to do personal prayer terribly well. She printed this in the Sunday edition and it was a kind of liberation for me. I felt as if I had reclaimed my spiritual identity. The disclosure was very healing because it put my spirituality back into the public domain.

God Excels in Forgiveness

People who had known me for some time but hadn't known that side of me began to share their faith. People who had trouble with the institutional church found it helpful to talk to someone who had also been hurt by it. Some of my deepest pain has come from the way the institutional church so easily writes people off because they are women or married priests or have a different sexual orientation. When I received my dispensation from celibacy in order to marry in the church, I was shocked to find that I would no longer be welcome to read scripture publicly in church or to serve in many public ministries. I wondered if the sacrament of marriage was going to thwart my ability to proclaim God's word. My wife, Carrie, and I were insulted and felt a deep sense of rejection. I believe that rejection is the most painful human experience. Silent prayer is gradually helping me to forgive even the harshness of the institutional aspects of the church. We humans are experts in anger; thankfully, God excels in forgiveness. This is a recent miracle in my life!

The Ecumenism of Meditation

I have always been a person with friends from many faiths. This led to an invitation to help facilitate a meditation group as a guest in the United Church in southern Alberta. It seemed that God was calling me to find the ever-elusive community by helping in the United Church. We met once a week for six weeks and it was a marvellous privilege. For two or three days early in the course, I went to the mountains for reflection before continuing with the group. One morning, I saw a beautiful wildflower by the edge of a stream and wrote a poem about it. Reflective writing is a new experience for me that has grown out of meditating. The poem, entitled "Revealing Beauty," was published in the September 1994 Canadian Christian Meditation Newsletter.

I took a picture of this simple little flower and shared copies of it with the people in the meditation course on the last evening of our gathering. One woman broke down in tears, saying that this was the type of flower her recently deceased grandpa had given to her grandma every spring on their farm near the mountains. The work of the Spirit!

The Fruits of the Spirit

The fruits of the Spirit are listed in Galatians 5:22 – love, joy, peace, patience, goodness, trustfulness, gentleness and self-control. Earlier in my life, I had a fair amount of anger. After a Sunday evening series on meditation I gave in Lent 1995, the evaluation forms said, "Tom's gentle way of teaching was very helpful." My daughter, Megan, who is grown up now recently told me that when she was young, she remembers that I would often retreat to my room for a "quiet time." (I was in fact meditating.) She said that she and my son, Ryan, learned that their dad was much more reasonable to deal with afterwards if he was not interrupted and had finished his quiet time. This was the beginning of the subtle changes in my life and, I think, had a profound impact on parenting patience.

Meditation Deepens Relationships

In the last few years, it seems that "when two or three gather" is characteristic of my journey in search of community. Carrie has joined me every morning for meditation for the past eight years. It has deepened our relationship. It gives both of us a unique perspective on what used to be perceived as day-to-day problems of parenting or discussions about finances. We simply love each other more deeply with the experience of meditation on which to build our relationship. What could be better for a marriage?

Another group of three meets in my office on Mondays at 4:44 before going home from work. I also meditate with a friend at 6:30 PM every Wednesday, before he goes off to his busy day at the hospital and I go for an early swim. Our friendship is close and we agree that much is shared in silence. Silence, like a picture, seems to say so much! In silence there is no need to impress the other, to put on a mask. We are connected in silence to Jesus, the author of love, and we are free to *be*, simply as we are, without demands to live up to anyone else's expectations. Community is being created in my heart through meditation and I have learned that we are called to *create* community.

Living Waters of Meditation

There was another marvellous "coincidence" that led me to ask, *Who takes the initiative?* At a national gathering of meditators in Victoria in May 1997, I was asked to share some thoughts on the fruits of meditation and the relationship between action and meditation. We spent a moment reflecting on God's living water, the source of contemplative energy for our action. We then drank some sparkling water quietly and reverently. Later, a woman from Manitoba, who ironically had left the great Manitoba flood on a train that didn't have any water, explained her experience. She said, "I truly was spiritually thirsty, and now I realize that I must have come to Victoria to experience this living water of meditation." She stated that she found this to be a very beautiful eucharist. This was quite healing for me. Rejection is fading in such love.

Thank you, Lord, for the peace and the beautiful relationships I have had the privilege to form with the people I have prayed with in silence. Thank you, Lord, for taking the initiative and enticing me to respond now twice a day. I love your silent love! I can now smile and just *be*.

Maurie Costello

Maurie Costello, 56, an orthodontist, is married to Glenda and lives in Rockhampton, Queensland, Australia. He has four adult children and one grandson. He is interested in ecumenism, and is a member of his Bishop's Ecumenical Commission and a Catholic representative on the local Rockhampton "Churches Together" ecumenical body. He is an avid fan of Bede Griffiths and collects a wide range of spiritual books as a hobby.

I was born in 1941 and received an excellent Catholic education with the Good Samaritan nuns and the Christian Brothers. Of course that was pre-Vatican II, and one's spirituality was full of a God of fear and a life of avoiding sin!

I can recall four distinct spiritual milestones in my adult life. My first adult spiritual awakening came in 1965, when I was posted to Malaysia as a dental officer with the Royal Australian Airforce. This was my introduction to Eastern spirituality. In Malaysia, Singapore, Thailand and Japan, I began visiting Hindu temples, Chinese shrines and Muslim mosques and reading about their philosophies.

I was surprised when a local Christian Brother in Penang showed me his college's religious education syllabus. Studies in Animism, Hindu Vedas and Upanishads, Sufi Spirituality, Chinese Tao and Buddhist Philosophy as well as the regular Christian doctrine were all covered in depth and with considerable understanding.

However, Malaysia was a multi-religious community and Christian Brothers were training young boys for their future life within their own culture. I found it an eye-opener. I then saw clearly how the Holy Spirit was at work in *all* the major religious traditions of the world. I experienced monks and lay people practising meditation in Malaysia but it was of academic interest to me rather than a personal awakening. It was to be another 30 years before the meditation seed finally germinated.

A God Within and a God of Nature

My second true awakening was meeting Glenda, my future wife, in 1967. I had a strong devotion, from my mother, to Our Lady of Perpetual Help, and spent many prayerful hours reflecting on this wonderful young lady I had just met. Her Christian spirituality was of a God *within*, and a God of *nature*, and was not bound by the structures of an institutional church. For Glenda, God was easily and directly approached and worshipped. We married one year later to the day, on May 24, 1968.

The years went by. In 1982 I attended a course on "Renewal of Faith" in our local parish. It was then I realized that I was a Christian through and through, and that my particular version of Christianity was Catholic. Up until then I believed that there were only two types of Christians: Catholics and non-Catholics. How narrow we were back then! Thus began my awakening interest in ecumenism.

The Charism of Bede Griffiths

My discovery of meditation came in 1994 when a close professional colleague, Dr. Glen Wolter, stayed with us during our city's Beef 94 Expo. (Rockhampton is the beef capital of Australia.) Glen lent me Bede Griffith's book *Ultimate Reality*; it transformed my life. After reading several of Bede's books I found many answers to my spiritual search for meaning. The ultimate reality is, after all, God: the life force, the creator, the Spirit, the nameless one, nirvana, etc., and it was through the practice of meditation that I discovered a method of attaining harmony with this reality.

Meditate One Day at a Time

My daily meditation has been quite a struggle, and at times I have faltered and given up for weeks, but whenever this happens I feel an almost ceaseless urge to start again. It is important not to load oneself with guilt, but merely to start again and treat *every* meditation as a fresh beginning. God does not keep count. To God each present moment is a sacrament in itself.

I encourage all those who are beginning to take heart and meditate one day at a time. It's not a race or a competition. It is merely opening our innermost being to the infinite love of our creator. In time, it becomes two very precious periods each day, wherein one can merely *be* in the presence of love flowing from the ultimate reality.

Four Local Christian Meditation Groups

Thanks to the encouragement and support of Bishop Brian Heenan, Catholic bishop of Rockhampton, we are fortunate to have four local Christian Meditation groups, providing a choice of six meetings each week. Most groups follow a standard John Main format, with a short taped talk by John Main followed by several minutes of music, then a 25-minute meditation. Informal discussion generally follows. There are up to 10 people in each group. I find the weekly meetings a real boost to my meditative journey. They provide me with the added incentive to keep meditating on a daily basis at home.

Tuning in to God's Creation

Until I began this practice of contemplative prayer my spiritual life was rather barren. In fact, I had entirely ceased all formal prayer. I now have an almost insatiable desire to read: scripture, poems, spiritual books, and even ones on quantum physics (yes, that's quite spiritual, too, especially the *silence* existing beyond the smallest particles of the atom, a world of *being*, energy and constant creation). Oh, what a tribute to God is modern science: the power, the planning, the coordination, the mystery! How could all this exist purely by chance?

Finally, I give a very special thank you to my colleague and mentor Glen Wolter. Glen introduced me to a wonderful method of centering and tuning in to God and the universe before each morning meditation session. Glen recommends facing East, opening one's arms wide and saying, "In the morning I greet Father, Son and Holy Spirit" (three times), "In the morning I greet Mother Earth and all her creatures" (three times), and "In the morning I greet all my brothers and sisters" (three times). What a way to tune into all God's creation before meditation! Thank you, Glen.

Patricia Gulick

Patricia Gulick is a mother of three adult children, and with her husband, Joseph, has been a member of St. Mary's Church, Ridgefield, Connecticut, USA, for the past 30 years. She has taught religious education in her parish, participated in the Rite of Christian Initiation of Adults and facilitated a bible study group. Patti is a weekly volunteer at the Dorothy Day House of Hospitality in Danbury, Connecticut, and she and Joe are active in the diocesan Cursillo movement. She is Christian Meditation coordinator (New England Region), is co-editor of the USA Christian Meditation newsletter, and runs her own weekly meditation group.

I have always felt a close relationship with God. Growing up in Essex Junction, Vermont, my sister Mary and I were devout little rascals. We were left on our own a great deal, because my father (a doctor) and my mother (his nurse) worked together in his office, which was located in our house. You literally went from the doctor's office into our kitchen. Mary and I said the rosary on our knees during our frequent visits to the nearby church, sometimes in our bedroom, or wherever the Spirit moved us to do so. Neither of us have ever gone through the current spiritual crisis of withdrawal from church or prayer.

In my adult and mothering years, I was attracted through my friends to the current spiritual trend or attention-getting focus of the time. I've learned to pray as charismatics do, attended Marian conferences at a shrine where alleged apparitions took place, and zeroed in when calamities struck people in Ridgefield, Connecticut, where I now live. I joined the Cursillo movement, and with my husband, Joe, participated in the perpetual eucharistic adoration program of St. Mary's parish. I've even experienced what might be called "a close encounter with the Lord." Why add anything else?

The Pull of the Spirit

What we all learn eventually is that the spiritual life is a journey. It is a journey of many facets. So it seems necessary to experience through life the pieces of the jigsaw puzzle that make up the richness of Christian life and relationships. In my case this entailed the traditionally proven, the present exigency, and an openness to the unceasing pull of the Spirit.

It was after this "close encounter" that I sought out a priest to be my spiritual director. He had recently begun a Christian Meditation group in his parish and invited me to attend. I went the next Thursday night, and have been meditating with this group for five years. I began going to St. Theresa parish in Trumbuli, a 45-minute ride from where I live, with two other interested friends. Since that time, both of these women have become leaders of Christian Meditation groups in their own parishes in different towns. I attend both of their groups as often as I can. Since Christian Meditation is the prayer of the heart, the love generated spills out in all directions.

On Involvement with Groups

In fact, in our geographically small diocese, we have evening meditation groups on Monday, Tuesday, Thursday and Friday, which offers meditators flexibility. There is also a Friday morning group meeting at a nursing home, conducted by residents. My father-in-law is a member of that group and began meditating last year at age 85!

I attend the other groups whenever I can. Through deeper prayer I have come to know what Fr. John Main taught and his successor Fr. Laurence continues to reiterate: Prayer is what binds us together, what makes us *one*. We do not come together as community merely to socialize. We come to pray in union and solidarity. We come to share our poverty and become rich in the Lord. This deeper and broader understanding of community has led me to an enriched dimension of the spiritual pilgrimage.

A Meditation Centre, "Patti's Patch"

One small building on our American-Revolution-period property had originally been a stable. Several years ago I converted it into an antique shop called "Patti's Patch." After I began to meditate, I turned it into a meditation centre, complete with prayer pillows, benches, chairs, etc. My husband and I meditate on Friday evenings there with whoever shows up.

Three years ago, in October, I sponsored what became "A Gathering of Meditators" at my home and Patti's Patch. I invited meditators from groups throughout Connecticut and New York to meditate and share a meal. Each year at these sessions, following meditation, Fr. Peter De Marco gives a 20-minute presentation on prayer and the spiritual life, which usually leads to some group discussion. Then everyone heads for the house for a delicious potluck supper. What has emerged is a spontaneous linking of meditation and a bonding with meditators from different areas. To me, this is what community is all about.

Community always leads to more community. My husband and I bought our retirement home in Ludlow, Vermont. Friends of my spiritual director have been practising Christian Meditation there and had begun the home meditation group upon which we in Connecticut modelled ours. I meditate with the Vermont group each time I visit and am accepted as one of their members. This past year I joined them when they observed the seventh anniversary of the group. Since they meet at the same time as the St. Theresa group in Connecticut, we are like sister-groups and think of each other as we pray each week.

Dorothy Day House of Hospitality

One of my great surprises in meditation happened at the Dorothy Day House of Hospitality in Danbury, Connecticut, where I volunteer each Tuesday afternoon. This is a soup kitchen which feeds homeless and needy guests for lunch and includes an adjacent building which houses a shelter in the evening. Like most other shelters, the common practice is that the guests must vacate the shelter early in the morning and cannot re-enter until about nine o'clock in the evening. The social worker at the house wanted to open the soup kitchen rooms in the evening so that the homeless residents of the shelter would have a warm place to wait until opening time.

She asked me if I would do something with them on Tuesday evenings, such as a session of Scripture reading or prayer. I decided to meditate with them in one of the two rooms. We play soft music, a John Main cassette tape, and put the lights out. We meditate for about 15 minutes. The lights from the street lamps outside give some illumination, and the sounds of the city street bombard the silence within. But we meditate. There is absolute seriousness and stillness. After the first meeting, as they helped me carry out the tape recorder and prayer cushions, the new meditators asked if I was coming back next week!

Not a Spiritual Trend

I do not consider myself to be following a spiritual trend, waiting until something else comes along. Everything in my whole life that enables a relationship with Christ and community as I understand it is good. The Lord makes it clear that a good tree is known by its fruits. The path of meditation has become my daily spiritual practice, with Christ as its cornerstone. So as this way of contemplative prayer has been from the time of the early Christians, and will be through the new millennium, so it is for me.

Seeing the Reality of Who I Am

Persistence and faithfulness in meditation and the community it creates have changed me. Family members have told me that I am more patient and tolerant. I recognize that my own attitudes have changed. I relate more to people's brokenness, try to affirm what is good in them, and acknowledge that we are all the same in our goodness, weakness and vulnerability. I am assuming a more nurturing, motherly role. This enhanced perspective may be the effect of more clearly seeing who I really am. I do not need, as we say in Vermont, to "make my face perfect," always looking over my shoulder, trying to live up to an image of who people think I should be. Now on the pilgrimage of meditation I can just be Patti.

Leon Milroy

Leon Milroy, an Australian, is married and has a 23-year-old son. She is a Catholic and has been involved over the years in a number of forms of prayer. She was a member of the Legion of Mary for five years, and is involved in the St. Vincent de Paul Society. A trained nurse, she has just completed a B.A. (Honours) in classical civilizations and has now started a Master's (Honours) degree, doing research studies in religions and prayer in early Christianity, Greco-Roman times and Judaism.

I am a beginner in Christian Meditation. I was first introduced to the practice of meditation by my Buddhist brother about 15 years ago. He converted to Buddhism from Catholicism during his university years and wanted me to share in the benefits he had found in meditation. But I was resistant to being taught anything that I thought was un-Christian. He did succeed, however, in making known to me the teaching of Buddhist meditation. It seemed useful as a tool for relaxing but, being a staunchly traditional Catholic, I could not bring myself to practise regularly what seemed to be a non-Christian form of prayer.

A Half-Hearted Commitment

My first experience of Christian Meditation was a day of renewal at the Benedictine monastery in Arcadia, New South Wales, in 1988. This was a day for beginners and other meditators and I was so enthusiastic at the apparent simplicity of it that I decided there and then that this was the way of prayer for me. I couldn't have listened very well to the speaker because when I went home I slotted in only one period, each morning, for meditation. I attended Mass daily but other types of prayer, such as meditation, were secondary and, of course, ones I practised only if I felt like it at the time. So I soon stopped meditating.

As I thought I knew all about it, I naively felt I could pick it up again at any time. I realize now that I had only made a half-hearted commitment to meditation, and despite its simplicity I found it very difficult to discipline myself. By telling myself I could only fit in one period a day I certainly wasn't being true to the discipline according to Dom John Main's teaching.

Over the years I joined fledgling groups where everyone was learning to meditate. I still must have been half-hearted because the necessity of meditating morning and evening each day still did not dawn on me. Perhaps I rationalized that I was too busy to do more than one period.

A Buddhist Led Me to the Practice

Last year, again because of my brother, I became interested in a full commitment to meditation. He had been preparing his home for a Buddhist meditation retreat and I was helping him by painting some furniture. My brother's commitment to the practice of Buddhist meditation was total. His example showed me that if one wishes to meditate, the practice has to be at the forefront of one's life. Partly in competition and partly in a desire to protect my Christian principles, I decided to commit myself to practising Christian Meditation seriously. This time I had two periods timetabled into my day, morning and evening, and I made an effort to find out more about it through the books and tapes of John Main and Laurence Freeman.

My sister-in-law, who had continued meditating following her first encounter with it 10 years earlier when we went together to the talks in Arcadia, also advised me to subscribe to the Australian Christian Meditation community newsletter and their lending library. She has encouraged me greatly by sending me information and urging me to meditate with her when we visit.

From Illusion to Reality

My spiritual path and daily life have changed greatly. Even though I am still a beginner each day and greatly distracted, my twice-daily meditation is the key point of my life. This practice has stimulated my faith. I know now that I had been living in illusion before starting to meditate.

About two years ago my husband and I moved from near Sydney to an inland rural area of New South Wales. It is halfway between Sydney and Brisbane, which are each six-and-a-half hours away. It is very isolated and the closest meditation group was about 100 kilometres away and took place at night. I was overjoyed when I discovered I could use my computer to contact other meditators who were on-line. My enthusiasm for everything to do with Christian Meditation led me to get in touch with Greg Ryan in New Jersey, USA. I wanted to start a meditation group in a nearby town and needed assistance on how to go about it. I saw Greg's e-mail address in the Newsletter and after I had accessed the World Wide Web I found I could now contact other meditators this way. I found the WCCM Web Page to be a great resource; Greg also put my name down on the Internet Weekly Meditation group. The weekly readings have been a great help in the meditation group I started in October 1997. I print out the readings and give them to the others. Through the Internet, I also became interested in becoming an oblate.

The eucharist and meditation in my life are what keep my spiritual life going. There have been times in my life when I have felt that I was going around in circles and that life was unreal. Meditation is now the reality in my life. It helps me appreciate life and creation. It is strange, but when I am meditating I feel a sense of freedom. Along with Mass, my morning and evening sessions are the most important times of my day.

The Group Has Deepened My Commitment

The meditation group that I started in Armidale, a town about 20 kilometres away, is small but enthusiastic. I think that, by starting the group, my commitment to meditation has deepened. I also listen to tapes by John Main or Laurence Freeman while driving to and from work, to the university or the group, and am always amazed at the freshness of their message no matter how many times I listen to their words.

When I first started meditating I listened to one of the 12 talks for meditators from John Main's *Essential Teaching* tape before every meditation period morning and evening for many weeks. I absorbed these basic guidelines and this assisted my resolution to keep meditating. As another practical aid, I printed a sign stating the time of my morning and evening meditation and display it on the door of my meditation room. This way, when I close the door to meditate I am not disturbed by anyone. I put another sign on the fridge. I was surprised recently when my son reminded me that it was my meditation time!

It's Meditation Time

My husband has always been supportive and encourages me to meditate. He has seen a change in my attitude to life. Perhaps he is happy for a bit of peace when I am meditating! The sign is also a means of letting visitors know about meditation, even though we don't get many in this isolated area. My sister-in-law also had a sign printed, and says that she finds it acts as a useful buffer from the many family requests that would otherwise interrupt her when she meditates.

One thing I find intriguing is that when the time for meditation draws near, Our Lord never lets me forget the truth of John Main's words that God issues the invitation to meditation: *"You did not choose me, I chose you."* (John 15:16)

Marlene Sweeney

Marlene Sweeney and her husband, Tim, live in Hanover Park, Illinois, USA. They are the parents of five children ranging in ages from 15 to 27. Marlene is a writer, poet and contemplative who has published numerous works in both books and periodicals. She is employed as the Director of Spiritual Formation at Transfiguration Parish in Wauconda, Illinois.

Several years ago I began visiting the Christian Meditation Center in Roselle, Illinois, on a regular basis. At the time I was a full-time graduate student trying to balance studies, raise five children, work part-time, and minister in my parish. It often seemed as if life couldn't hold one more thing: that is, until I discovered meditation. In the midst of thesis writing, laundry and daily demands on my time, I would leave my home at noon and fall into the arms of a waiting God.

"Meditation Makes Doing Nothing 'Respectable'"

Incorporating meditation into my busy life has allowed silence to take root in me. I jokingly tell my family that meditation makes doing nothing "respectable." But truly, I've experienced a new way to grow closer to the Lord and a new way to pray. Prayer is not always talking to God, but just being with him as well. I can see that this regular discipline is leading me to a new depth of listening with the heart and revealing the holy within.

Meditation can transform our busy lives if we allow it to. The great thing about it is that you don't have to make anything happen; all you have to do is show up!

Before I discovered meditation, I felt I had been working on my prayer life for most of my adult years. I did work on it: another good book on prayer, a bible course, a faith-sharing group, etc. Although all these tools helped me know God better and gave me language to converse with others about him, I still sensed a deeper call.

I wanted to move away from the wish-list praying that I often experienced. I felt a need to move my prayer life out of the many cerebral activities I undertook every day and to experience God in a more skin-to-skin way. At about this time a friend invited me to the Meditation Center. She assured me that all I had to do was show up.

Without knowing, I opened myself up to the possibility of doing nothing and, surprisingly, God filled the void. In the emptiness, I grew aware of a deeper sense of God within. Slowly, I became comfortable with just showing up.

The God of the Present Moment

I can assure you, acquiring the discipline of showing up has taken time. Learning to be still, silent and open to God in the present moment is a daily struggle, given the fast-paced society we live in. However, over time, I have recognized the transforming life experience of meditation. As I develop a daily routine of quiet, I recognize God within. I find myself deepening my attention and awareness of his presence in all aspects of my life. The God of the present moment has broken out of the confines of the Christian Meditation Center and I'm learning to carry him in all that I do. Now, as I look back on this evolving process I realize how all of this "becoming" has helped me come to this day.

A Mind on Information Overload

I am a full-time Director of Spiritual Formation in an active, vibrant parish of 2,300 families. I still have all the busyness and responsibilities of home. The demands on my day have not lessened from seven years ago, when I was first introduced to meditation. I seldom have the luxury of visiting the Christian Meditation Center at noon anymore, as I work 20 miles away. However, the gift of meditation carries me through most days.

My life could easily be a whirlwind of activity, filled with comings and goings, every calendar space marked with community events, meetings, and other worthwhile activities. Couldn't all our lives reflect countless days filled with endless activities?

When my mind is on information overload I find comfort in one of my favourite scripture quotes: *"I came so that you may have life and have it abundantly."* (John 10:10) Not merely that you may survive!

Living a full and responsible life while maintaining a close relationship with the Lord is a challenge for all adults in our fast-paced culture. Thank goodness I have discovered the one tool that works for me.

Attending to God

The word "meditation" comes from the Latin word *mederi*, which means "to attend to." It is in allowing myself the quiet, empty space in which God can dwell that I discover what it is I need to attend to. Anyone active in parish ministry knows that, in a given day, there are countless things one can attend to. Meditation allows me the unique advantage of attending to God. I needn't start my day with my "to do" list in order to do God's work. Instead I spend time in quiet emptiness, where God inspires, fills and accomplishes the ministry he sets before me. I have never done *more* while doing *less*.

Judi Taylor

Judi Taylor, who lives in New South Wales, Australia, is a 48-year-old mother of three children and the wife of Paul, with whom she shares the meditative journey. A social worker by training, she now works from home organizing talks and workshops for parents on various family-related topics. She and Paul lead three Christian Meditation groups in their parish.

I grew up the second of seven children in a strict Catholic family: weekly Mass, holy days, evening rosary, fasting on Fridays, the whole lot. Even as a child I sensed the negative weight of obligation in all of them. At the same time there were some ecstatic moments: occasionally during Mass or in my daily life, running on the rocks or climbing a tree. And from time to time I had a sense of fullness and joy at how life was unfolding. My childhood experiences have been and remain a kind of touchstone for me, and can guide me when I may be confused about how to understand something.

Leaving school and being able for the first time to choose, I angrily parted company with the church. University days and my early years of following my chosen career of social work confirmed this decision. It was a time of idealism and protest and great seriousness about where my life was headed.

A moment of truth came with hearing that first cry of my firstborn: an urgency, a realization that I had pushed aside and put on hold all questions of God and spirituality. Thus began an active 17-year search to find a way to express my relationship to the divine other. I learned to meditate with an Indian teacher, and for some years was part of a school which aimed at inner transformation.

A Sense of Connection

About five years ago I heard tapes of the talks given by Laurence Freeman in Sydney in 1992 and immediately experienced a sense of connection with this spiritual way. That grew into a great joy at finding such riches coming out of the faith of my childhood. It was a coming home. That joy remains. Love, intelligence and a strong sense of being have replaced the oppressive obligation of my childhood encounters. Yes, meditation is a daily discipline, and the onus is on me to be faithful to the tradition.

Room to Be Who I Am

And then, somehow, I found myself reconnecting with the Church. A real miracle after such anger, distance and alienation. I wonder at the power of my mother's prayer! I now have a wonderful parish and priest, and freedom and room to be who I am and to follow the path that is right for me. So many people in the parish are passionate about their relationship with Christ, which is a real source of sustenance in their lives. That, of course, creates community.

This is a journey shared with Paul, my husband, and now we run three meditation groups in the parish and try to understand and live out the truly radical call of the gospel. Many worlds have been opened to me on this journey of meditation. I have grown up and I now have a sense of intimacy and friendship with Jesus. I've also found a deepening interest in knowing myself and a willingness to accept unpalatable aspects of myself. In this, the study of the Enneagram has seemed a natural companion to meditation. More recently, my awareness of social justice issues has expanded. I have felt drawn imperceptibly into action, and wish to be part of the reconciliation process with our Aboriginal people. I want to share with them the listening – *dadirri* – that is of the Spirit.

Truly my life in all its joy and difficulty reflects the promise of richness I glimpsed as a child, and I thank God that I have been shown this way.

Chapter 6

Meditation and the Priesthood

"We Are All Beginners"

Frank Cassidy
Peter A. De Marco
Frank Delia
John Jay Hughes
Denis Mahony
Michael Mifsud
Henri Tardy
Seraphim Thomas
David Wood

Frank Cassidy

Fr. Frank Cassidy has been a priest of the Los Angeles archdiocese for over 40 years. He was ordained at All Hallows Seminary, Dublin, Ireland, in 1959. His entire ministry in the priesthood has been in parish work; he has had assignments at eight different parishes.

During my years as a seminarian studying for the priesthood, I was told many times by spiritual directors that meditation was the highest form of prayer. The first half hour every morning in church was designated as time for meditation. Unfortunately, no one seemed to know how to teach the way of meditation. Some books on the subject were recommended to us, but the books were not enough. We needed more. As a result, we never learned to meditate.

"This Man Speaks with Authority"

I've been a priest for over 40 years. About 12 years into the priesthood I started to develop an interest in meditation as a result of some reading I was doing at the time. That interest continued through the years. I tried different ways of meditation. Each method was a help. In 1981 somebody handed me a tape by Dom John Main. I listened to it. I remember being struck by the unique sense of authority in his voice. I was reminded of what the people said of Jesus in the New Testament: *"This man speaks with authority and not like the scribes."* (Matthew 7:29) I resolved to hold onto the tape, even though I didn't listen to it again for some years.

A weekly prayer group that started in the parish was seeking the direction of a priest, and I was assigned to the task. They were interested in the prayer of silence. John Main's tape came to mind. I used it to help them, not knowing it was going to make a big impact on me. I bought more of his tapes and books. Before long I was into his daily way of meditation. I stopped and re-started a number of times along the way. Now *Maranatha* has become my permanent way.

Starting a Meditation Group

I moved to my present parish in 1988. Within two years of my arrival I started a John Main meditation group. We've been meeting consistently once a week for eight years now. We have 10 to 15 regulars every week; many more have come and gone through the years. That weekly meeting is such a boost to me. The stillness created by the group, together in meditation, is extraordinary. It is truly sacred. It recharges me for the whole week.

I seem to greet the problems I encounter through the week less with resistance and more and more with the cushion of the silence that my being taps into daily through meditation. In our weekly meeting we move from the silence of the first 45 minutes to a 40-minute discussion on a spiritual topic, and then to an actual laying on of hands with some short traditional prayer. I find the movement from silence to discussion to the laying on of hands to be unifying and enriching. Our meeting lasts a little over two hours and never seems too long.

John Main's tapes are such a treat. His explanation of St. Paul's thought is very inspiring. And Laurence Freeman does a magnificent job of continuing where John Main left off. *Maranatha* is a great gift and I feel blessed to have been invited to respond to its call.

The Sacred Word Beyond Thoughts

Various insights have come to me as I stayed with the path of meditation. Alcoholics Anonymous says that in recovery one must "not try to think his/her way into right action but instead act his/her way into right thinking." It seems to me that this is what we do in meditation. The saying of the sacred word is an action that is designed to take us beyond thoughts and, as we stay with that action through the days and months, a new way of thinking is gradually given to us by the Holy Spirit. So, through our daily discipline we act our way into right thinking.

Meditation and Negative Emotions

I've also gained some insight into negative emotions, especially guilt. Many people are plagued by guilt and much of it is false. They never seem to be able to get beyond it. The discipline of daily meditation offers a wonderful way to handle guilt or other lingering negative emotions.

The advice given for handling distraction in meditation can be usefully applied to our dealing with unwanted emotions. Just as when we notice the distraction in our prayer we gently return to the mantra, so also when we notice unwanted emotions appearing in our day we quietly return to whatever task we have at hand. We learn in meditation how not to be hooked by the distraction; so also we can learn through our day how not to be hooked by negative emotions. Of course I strongly believe that the saying of the mantra opens the door for extraordinary work to be done unconsciously within us by the Holy Spirit by eliminating all negativity.

Practising the Presence of God

John Main says that meditation is a practice of learning to focus on a God who is continually focused on us. As we stay with the discipline we become more present to God, to the moment and to our sisters and brothers. A popular book in Catholic circles has been Brother Lawrence's classic *Practising the Presence of God*. I see the daily saying of the mantra as a wonderful way of practising the presence of God. Fr. William McNamara O.C.D., the founder of the Nova Nada contemplative community, says that the spiritual journey is a discipline of learning to become personally, passionately present to a God who is personally, passionately present to us. I believe that this is what happens to us daily as we, through our mantra, learn to focus more deeply on God.

"We Do Not Know How to Pray"

These two statements from the New Testament point to our helplessness in spiritual matters. One is by Jesus: *"Without me you can do nothing"* (John 15:5); the other is by St. Paul: *"We do not know how to pray as we ought but the Spirit within us knows how to pray."* (Romans 8:26) I feel that many people get discouraged as they endeavour to walk the spiritual path because they try to do it their way. Our way never works. Only God's way does. The daily saying of the mantra is a practice in learning to let him do it. I feel that, as we sit to say our word, we are like Mary before the Angel, saying: *"Let it be done unto me according to your word."* (Luke 1:38) Mary didn't know what the Angel meant but trusted the process and extraordinary things happened. Likewise, we put our faith in the saying of our word and great things happen in and through us. It is all grace. It is all gift. How privileged we are to be its beneficiaries.

Jesus said: *"I thank you, Father, because what you have hidden from the learned and the clever you have revealed to the merest children."* (Matthew 11:25) The saying of the mantra is not the way of learning and cleverness. It is the way of little children. And Jesus tells us that unless we become as little children we will not enter the kingdom of heaven.

How blessed we are!

Peter A. De Marco

Fr. De Marco is a native of Bridgeport, Connecticut. Throughout his priestly ministry he has been in parish work, except for short years in Special Education, ministering to the mentally challenged, blind and deaf for the diocese. He was pastor of St. Mary's Church in Bethel, Connecticut, for almost 12 years. He has also been Spiritual Director of the diocesan Cursillo movement. He now serves as associate pastor in a large suburban parish, working especially with the Rite of Christian Initiation of Adults and religious education of youth and adults. He has been with the World Community for Christian Meditation since 1995, and is coordinator for the US northeast region, co-editor of the US newsletter, and a member of the National Advisory Board.

What happens when a parish priest turns the corner on a quarter century of ministry and discovers he has a double dilemma? The first dilemma is that his life has become an unending schedule of activity. The second is that the prayer pattern bolstering his whole life is slipping into a pattern of routine and lip service.

This dual crisis of overextended activity and dead-in-the-sand spirituality occurred to me in the early 1980s. I strongly believed in the scriptural quote *"...for those who love God everything works out for good,"* (Romans 8:28) but I also knew deep down that I had better be ready for changes to take place.

"Why Say the Mantra from Beginning to End?"

One day I borrowed a set of cassettes from the diocesan tape library. It was Dom John Main's *Essential Teaching* series. Was it the English accent of this Benedictine priest that was so intriguing? I listened to his presentation of what meditation is and what its history has been, and I practised meditating with the 12 short talks Fr. Main presented. I found his talks to be convincing, and continued meditating in this manner for a short period of time. But it came to an end since I was doing it alone, without support, and was perturbed by a nagging question: "Why say the mantra from beginning to end?"

Some two years later, two longtime friends of mine in Ludlow, Vermont, began to mention John Main's name when I visited them. Joe and Angie Barcello had already discovered Fr. John and were following his meditation teaching. Each time we met, I challenged them with the same questions, especially about the mantra. They tried to explain, but more importantly they gave me the example of two lay people persisting in meditation, and later demonstrated the influence and support of the meditation group they formed.

Prayer Being Born in the Hearts of People Everywhere

In the summer of 1989 I made a weeklong retreat at the Benedictine Priory in Montreal. There I met and talked with Fr.

Laurence Freeman, the successor to Fr. John Main. It was there I saw in the flesh what I was beginning to read and hear: the desire for prayer being born in the hearts of people everywhere. Each day at this Priory in the midst of downtown Montreal, men and women of all ages came to meditate on their way to work, and returned to meditate in the chapel before returning to their homes. Praying with them convinced me that this is what I was looking for and what I needed to offset my busy life. It would become the means for God to reshape me.

Beginning a Group

I returned to the Montreal Priory the next summer for a month-long sabbatical. The teaching and practice took deeper root. I asked to begin the process of becoming a Benedictine oblate. I felt this would be another way to commit to prayer. When I returned to St. Theresa's parish in Trumbull, Connecticut, I spoke with some people already engaged in meditating, and after explaining John Main's teaching, asked if they would like to try this. This became the Christian Meditation group which met weekly in the home of Jeanette and Dante Pellei.

The Monk Within

Meditation has become the centrepiece of my spiritual life, like two pillars in the morning and evening, anchoring me to the Lord. My active ministry now moves between these pillars, for meditation enlightens everything I do with purpose and more coherence. In the spirit of St. Benedict, I strive to balance my active ministerial life with a focus on "the monk within." This includes daily eucharist in the local assembly and *lectio divina*, the prayerful reading of scripture. Silence becomes much more the norm throughout the day, painting action and prayer in surprising colour and depth. The day is planned around meditation, and only seldom does it become a matter of "fitting it in." I often notice that I have incorporated the monk's *ora et labora* in my life as a diocesan priest in the world, and now the day seems more balanced.

Five years ago, I felt that St. Theresa's parish would benefit from a meditation group that would be a source of teaching and practice of this way of prayer. Members of our original home group became the nucleus for the new one. Patti Gulick came a year later with Mary Jo Kumke and Silvana Saverezza, from towns 20 miles away. Today, each of them leads a meditation group. Patti also coordinates Christian Meditation in New England with me and is co-editor of the USA national newsletter.

"We Are Always Beginners"

So now, as a meditator, I am no longer alone. There are five groups close by meeting on different days. I have attended John Main seminars, as well as retreats and day-seminars by Fr. Laurence and Paul Harris. There is now a national advisory board, and new titles of books and tapes are added yearly to Fr. John's foundational teaching. My daily meditation continues with the years and yet, as Father John said and as those now teaching repeat, "We are always beginners." Priests, who are so often in the role of leader and presider at prayer times, the presumed teachers, are learners also.

Not long ago, three of our small diocesan priest prayer groups joined for an evening of prayer and camaraderie. We began in the parish church. The pastor placed the monstrance with the blessed sacrament upon the altar. He turned on a tape he had prepared with spiritual music, spacing each piece with a 15-minute interval of silence. Throughout, I said my "*Maranatha.*" We concluded the final five minutes with intercessory prayer. When the hour was concluded, we walked into the rectory for supper with a peace and joy shared by all 13 priests.

The rest of the evening was conspicuously lacking in the negative conversations and complaining that had so often been part of our clergy gatherings. The silence had stripped us of that outlet and, more than that, had bonded us into a group which could see the unity and purpose of our lives in Christ. Many said that night, "Let's do this again!"

Prayer Is Wrestling with the Angel

My active ministry is still busy; praying is always like Jacob wrestling with the angel. But I never neglect it. The daily practice of meditation is the boat cutting through the storms of this transitional era as we enter into the new millennium. The current seesaw period in the church makes for challenging sailing. There are times when the discouragement is sharper than the euphoria. I frequently recall Fr. Laurence's words to me at that Montreal retreat: "Keep praying, keep saying your word." I choose to do so. The rest is in the hands of God.

Frank Delia

Fr. Frank Delia is a Capuchin Friar who ministered in different parishes in India and Australia for 38 years. He lives in Malta, his home country, and promotes Christian Meditation in this island of St. Paul.

I consider Christian Meditation to be the most outstanding grace the Lord has granted me in the latter days of my life. I have prayed and searched for this form of contemplative prayer ever since I joined the Capuchin order. I had always looked at it as an ideal to be achieved on my spiritual path. Yet, I always thought of it as unattainable for ordinary Christians. I suffered from the illusion that only "special" souls could be chosen for such a gift.

I persisted in this common illusion until some years ago, when I was introduced to the teaching of Dom John Main. When I was in Perth, West Australia, I visited many charismatic prayer meetings in my capacity as liaison priest of Archbishop Foley. It was during one of these visits that I met Vesta Gamalatge, a leader of a meditation group, who spoke to me about meditation. The name of John Main was brought to my awareness for the first time. I must admit that I didn't pay much attention to it. Hence, I lost the golden opportunity of having my longstanding prayer answered. Thank heaven the opportunity was not lost forever. I received a second knock on the door.

Later I left Perth and moved to Malta for health reasons. Once, after holy communion, Vesta's image and invitation to meditation came like a flash to my mind. On the very same day I wrote to Vesta for more information and literature. Happily, I received these by return mail.

Dom John Main, My Spiritual Guru

Now I really became vitally interested in learning about this form of contemplative prayer. I went through all the papers she sent me in no time flat. Fortunately, a particular note drew my attention to Dom John Main in such a way that I was deeply impressed. This proved to be a decisive moment for me. Because of it I have held Dom John Main as my spiritual "guru" ever since.

John Main repeatedly said that the most important thing to know about meditation is how to meditate. These were inspiring words for me. Until then, I had striven to understand the *meaning* of contemplation. Now, I had found the key to understanding what it is all about; namely, learn how to do it and start doing it. Jump in and get wet.

"It Was Not So Easy After All"

I followed his advice. Encouraged and inspired by this new teacher, I read the guidelines he gave on how to meditate. Indeed, these seemed to be so simple that I could hardly believe anything could come out of them. I immediately started to meditate in this way. I sat down, closed my eyes, and tried to recite within the mantra he recommended: "*Maranatha.*" This was my first experience of this kind of prayer. It seemed to be simple and easy to follow, yet I found out that John Main was right in his warning that it was not so easy after all. Yet I was not discouraged and continued to do it daily in the morning and at night in 20-minute periods.

Keeping in mind this simple way of meditating, I embarked on a long pilgrimage that I hope will last until the end of my days on earth. I have never looked back and have rarely omitted this twice-daily spiritual discipline. Nevertheless, I have to admit that I haven't yet mastered it to any degree. It doesn't matter as long as I keep doing it. John Main teaches us not to give up *ever*.

The Struggle of the Daily Practice

This daily practice, though a struggle, has brought me to a great commitment and stricter discipline on the spiritual path. It has become my spiritual challenge and my daily way of prayer. This pilgrimage is leading me into a deeper consciousness about truths of our Christian faith. John Main's teaching is becoming clearer to me than ever before and many other blessings are being showered on me.

John Main says that talking about meditation is never sufficient. Nothing we say about meditation is ever satisfactory. How true this is. Yet I cannot help speaking about it and proclaiming it to all those who are hungry for God and who wish to mature even more in their loving relationship with the Lord.

Christians who devote themselves to this way of prayer will also develop a heightened interest in liturgical and communal prayer. Yet there is always a special taste for this silent, still and intensive union with the Lord in the deepest part of our being, and at these moments the truth of the Psalmist is verified: *"Be still and know that I am God."* (Psalm 46:10)

John Jay Hughes

John Jay Hughes is a priest of the St. Louis archdiocese. He has taught at universities on both sides of the Atlantic and has served as pastor of three parishes and in diocesan administration. He is the author of nine books, most recently, Pontiffs: Popes Who Shaped History *(Our Sunday Visitor and Gracewing, 1994).*

I was born in 1928, the son and grandson of priests in the Episcopal Church. The religion in which I was brought up from childhood was sacramental and altar-centred. You could call it Catholicism without the Pope. Until I was 12 my family lived in New York City, where my father was Precentor at the Cathedral of St. John the Divine. He would often take me with him when he celebrated a weekday Mass, trying to teach me the names of the vestments as he put them on in the Cathedral sacristy: amice, alb, cincture, maniple, stole and chasuble. To my father's openly expressed dismay, the only one my child's brain could retain was "stole," so I can hardly have been more than four years old.

It was a fascination with the church as a very human and deeply fallible institution which first drew me to priesthood, more than idealistic motives of service or evangelism. From an early age I listened, fascinated, to my father's conversations with colleagues about church affairs. Not that I was a stranger to idealism. But from the start (and to a large extent still) my idealism was channelled into what I would learn decades later was called the search for God. At the heart of the gospel is the good news that God is searching for us before we start searching for him. Francis Thompson expressed this truth in his great poem *The Hound of Heaven*, with its haunting opening lines:

> I fled him, down the nights and down the days;
> I fled him down the arches of the years...

The Search Begins

My own search began, consciously and in earnest, in my thirteenth year, when I made my first confession, a sacrament which is voluntary for Anglicans and used, as a rule, only by those who are especially pious or think they have been especially bad. I also joined what Catholics would call a sodality: the Servants of Christ the King. Members undertook to follow a rule of life: daily morning and evening prayer, grace before meals, weekly Mass and communion, monthly confession, observance of the Friday abstinence from meat, and on five days each week 10 minutes of mental prayer (discursive meditation, for which a little handbook containing the rule and prayers gave simple directions). Members graded their observance of this rule on a scale of one to 10 in an annual written report to the director, a monk of the Episcopal Order of the Holy Cross, and received a friendly note of admonition and encouragement in response.

It was faithfulness to this rule of mental prayer which gave me, at age 15, the closest thing to a religious experience I have ever had. In the summer of that year I had my first paid job, working in the photostat department of a Wall Street bank. During my lunch hour I always visited Trinity Church, on Broadway at the head of Wall Street. In the Blessed Sacrament chapel to the right of the high altar I made the daily meditation required by my rule of life.

Inner Joy and Peace

Kneeling there one day I became aware of the chorus of prayer and praise ascending at that moment from convent and monastery chapels all over the world to the God I too was struggling to worship. My prayer, so full of distractions and mostly so dry, was a tiny drop in a vast ocean.

That was all. There were no voices, no intense feelings, certainly nothing like a vision. But at the time it was very real to me and brought me inner joy and peace. More than a half-century of perseverance in prayer since then has brought me nothing more. For that I have no regrets. A wise and generous God has given me something better: unshakeable, rocklike faith. For those so blessed, religious experiences are superfluous.

The Practice of the Presence of God

Following my graduation from college I studied for three years at an Anglican seminary in England. In those years I read widely in the areas of ascetical and mystical theology: Teresa of Avila, John of the Cross, Francis de Sales, Abbot Marmion, Sister Elizabeth of the Trinity. I was especially impressed by a little classic that is hardly known to Catholics these days: *The Practice of the Presence of God*.

The author, a seventeenth-century French Carmelite, described how he remained always recollected as he presided over the kitchen in his Parisian monastery. If he could do it, why not I? *Constantly thinking about God* was, I realized, impractical. I decided to recall the presence of God during activities which did not require concentration. Finding the right one proved difficult. After several false starts I hit on the idea of remembering God's presence whenever I went up or down stairs, an activity which would recur throughout my life, until I was incapacitated by accident or illness. I decided to turn stairs into "times for God." After years of perseverance this practice has become habitual, a source of rich blessing and inner joy.

The Soul of the Apostolate

The book which made the strongest impression on me was *The Soul of the Apostolate* by the French Trappist Abbot Jean-Baptiste Chautard, first published in 1910. I reread it recently and found it in many ways dated. But its central theme is timeless: that Christian ministry of any kind is an exercise in futility unless it is firmly rooted in the solid and disciplined practice of prayer. Neglect of this fundamental truth is the root cause of much of the church's current malaise.

I have mentioned my own efforts at discursive meditation as a young teenager: using the imagination to picture a biblical scene, the mind to reflect on its meaning, and the will to make acts of faith, hope, love, repentance and thanksgiving. By age 20, when I entered the seminary, this form of prayer gave way to spiritual reading and reflection and, as the years went on, more and more to what the books call "affective prayer." "Don't let me get away, Lord," I would pray over and over again; and "Not what I want, Lord, but what you want."

My prayer has changed greatly since those far-off days when I struggled with discursive meditation. For close to two decades I practised daily the simple form of contemplative prayer known these days as "centering prayer." A little pamphlet which I wrote on the subject in 1981, mostly cribbed from the Trappists Basil Pennington and Thomas Keating, is now approaching 200,000 copies in print. (*Centering Prayer: How to Pray from the Heart*, Ligouri Publications, Ligouri, MO.)

Maranatha: Come, Lord Jesus

In the last decade, however, I have moved beyond the method described there to the prayer of the mantra taught by John Main and propagated worldwide today by his disciple Laurence Freeman. For a half-hour before Mass each day I sit repeating with every heartbeat the separate syllables of the prayer-word: "*Maranatha,*" (Come, Lord Jesus). Do I have wandering thoughts, distractions? Of course: all the time! I count myself still a rank beginner in prayer. I find, however, that this time spent waiting in silence on the Lord nourishes me. Where, years ago, 20 minutes seemed long, a half-hour now seems too short. I am disappointed when I hear the deacon in the sacristy and know I must break off.

The Liturgy with Reverence and Awe

The Mass which follows my meditation is literally the high point of my day: it is "sunshine" as the St. Louis liturgical pioneer Msgr. Martin Hellriegel used to say. I was moved a few years back to read some words of an English priest on his fiftieth anniversary of ordination:

> I was new to the priesthood when a wise old canon told me that the influence that most moved the people to sanctity was how Mass was said.... A liturgy which has aptness, form, and reverence at the close makes real the presence of the Holy.

Celebrating the liturgy with reverence and awe is, I am convinced, the best service we can give our people. We can do this, however, only if we are people of prayer. Let me conclude with some words of the late Tom Burns, long-time editor of the London *Tablet*:

Those who have had the fortune to travel widely and meet priests in many countries will agree that, though they may have met embittered and frustrated men here and there, for the most part their encounter has been with dedicated men: unselfish to a degree, simple and honest and above all happy in their vocation. Such travellers must ask themselves if they can say the same of all their married friends.

Priests would give different reasons for this happiness. For me the supreme reason is the privilege, so far beyond anyone's deserving, of offering daily the sacramental memorial of the one, full, perfect and all-sufficient sacrifice of Calvary; and being nourished by, and distributing to the Lord's holy people, that daily bread for which Jesus taught us to pray.

Denis Mahony

Denis Mahony is a Marist priest from New Zealand who has worked in Papua New Guinea and Fiji in parishes, in seminary and in religious formation. At present he is a member of a Marist Contemplative Community at a prayer centre in Fiji and has been instrumental in the start-up of a dozen Christian Meditation groups in this area of the South Pacific.

Forty years ago, as I began my journey into religious life, I was taught what was called mental prayer with the promise that if I remained faithful to it, it would sustain me throughout my religious and priestly life. Apart from this initial teaching in prayer, there was little follow-up in the years after that and I was left to my own resources. For the next 20 years I endeavoured to be faithful to the daily period of mental prayer, but more and more it became a burden. I read many books on prayer and tried different methods but this daily exercise became more difficult and I resorted mostly to saying vocal prayers.

I first heard of Christian Meditation in the early 1980s when someone lent me one of John Main's books, *Word into Silence*. I knew at once that I had discovered something I had been looking for through all the years. It immediately struck a chord deep within me. I read the book several times, and began to meditate using the mantra. John Main's book seemed to be written just for me. Before returning it to the person who had lent it to me, I typed out several chapters so I could keep referring to them. I did not know anything about John Main or of the growth of Christian Meditation, but I continued to pray this way for about the next 10 years.

This prayer was never easy and there were many doubts, but it seemed right and I persevered. I was not getting any great "light" in prayer but I had an inner peace and I discovered the scriptures in a new way. They started to come alive for me. It would have been very helpful during these years to have had the support of a group or other meditators, but at the time I did not know of their existence. Finally, years later, I again heard of John Main and learned that he had written other books on Christian Meditation.

The Australian Christian Meditation Network

Ten years after my first introduction to John Main I was appointed to the Nazareth Prayer Centre, where I now live. I had been here only a short while when a woman named Irene Koroi came to spend some time in prayer. She showed me a copy of *Christian Meditation Network,* the Australian Christian Meditation quarterly newsletter, which opened up a whole new world to me. I had no idea of the existence of meditation groups and the network of meditators all over Australia and around the world. In this issue there was an inspiring letter by Dom Laurence Freeman, book reviews, news from meditation groups from all the states of Australia and the addresses of the coordinators of these groups.

Irene, who had come into contact with a meditation group while visiting Australia, asked if a group could be started in Fiji. I went through the names of the Australian coordinators and by a happy choice I wrote to Kate Thomas in Victoria, asking for help and advice. Kate replied immediately, warmly, lovingly and sent a booklet on how to start a meditation group. A few weeks later

Irene and I invited a few others to join us and we started the first group of Christian Meditators in Fiji.

The Importance of the Group Meeting

Today, there are 12 groups around the country. We have been generously helped in spreading the good news of Christian Meditation by meditation groups in Canada and Australia and by Bob Lukey, the librarian for the Australian Meditation Community. These wonderful people have become our good friends. In 1995 and again in 1997 we sponsored a series of talks by Paul Harris to meditators and those showing some interest. These talks were an inspiration and a great boost to our meditators. I have become convinced of the importance of the group meeting to pray together in silence and to listen to one of Fr. Main's talks, which are so steeped in scripture. I find his authoritative but gentle manner always reassuring and encouraging. It seems that no matter how many times I listen to the tapes I learn something new.

In 1994 another Marist priest and I were given approval to begin a small apostolic contemplative community at the Prayer Centre. There is now a permanent core community which endeavours to live and witness to the essential contemplative aspect of the Christian life while creating at the Prayer Centre a place/space/presence where others may come to experience God. The community emphasizes in its daily program the contemplative values of prayer, simplicity and silence, and invites those who come to the Centre to enter into the life and spirit of the community. Last year there were two religious sisters, a religious brother, a lay woman and me in the core community.

Sharing the Teaching in Fiji

Sr. Denise McMahon SMSM became a member of our core community in 1998. Although the Prayer Centre is very small, during the last 12 months nearly 1,400 people joined the community for varying lengths of time for retreats, days of recollection and the like. Many left with an experience of contemplation; some, I know, continue to practise it in their daily lives. I am now responding to invitations from different groups in Fiji to introduce them to Christian Meditation and to answer this growing hunger for prayer, especially among the laity.

In my early years I had the misconception that contemplative prayer was the preserve of the few, an elite specially called by God, people who usually lived in monasteries. Rereading the documents of Vatican II and the writings of Frs. John Main and Laurence Freeman, I came to understand that *all* God's people are called to the fullness of the Christian life and to the perfection of charity. Fr. John has re-articulated the Vatican II imperative that all are called to contemplative prayer and has given the contemporary world a simple, but not always easy, way to pray contemplatively. I have a great desire to share this gift with others and to help them become aware of the treasure that lies within.

Michael Mifsud

> *Fr. Michael Mifsud lives as a hermit in the state of Victoria, Australia, under the authority of the Archbishop of Melbourne. He was born in Malta, emigrated with his family to Australia at the age of four, and felt from an early age an attraction both to the priesthood and to the contemplative monastic life. He is now affiliated with the Carmalodese Benedictines, Big Sur, California, USA. Although he lives alone, his hermitage is open to others and he ministers and give retreats from time to time. He lives simply and close to the earth, growing vegetables, walking, reading, meditating, writing and receiving visitors.*

Hardly knowing what it is, I was, from an early age in primary school, always drawn to the mystery of prayer. It was a vague yet persistent calling of God: to interiority, to a silent awareness of a mystery apprehended in nature, in the Mass, in the haunting Gregorian chant, and in the lives of missionary monks like Boniface that the nuns used to read to us about.

As a student, I found adoration of the Blessed Sacrament and the example of the lives of the saints drew me to a deeper, prayerful union with God. Also as a teenager I came across the plight of the Dalai Lama and Tibetan people in the 1960s. Their spiritual and monastic lives drew me deeply with compassion into the mystery of the Spirit. Their ceaseless mantra "Om mani padme hum" even then impressed itself on my heart and mind.

I was very heartened when I entered the diocesan seminary to find an old Jesuit priest extolling the benefit of repetitive prayer as a means of letting prayer get deeper into our unconscious mind and then into our heart. Also within my first year there I began reading Thomas Merton, and I came across the Tarrawarra Cistercian Abbey not far away. Both these influences strengthened my commitment to meditation and broadened its horizons.

The Jesuits taught us their method of discursive meditation but also in my time they pointed to the Carmelite and Benedictine traditions of prayer.

Contemplative Prayer in the 1960s

So, from the late 1960s I was using the mantra and silent prayer as a regular feature of my growth in Christian Meditation. Soon I came across the books of William Johnston, SJ, and Henri Le Saux, OSB, and gradually became more disciplined in both mantric and silent meditation. I was especially drawn to being in the presence of the Blessed Sacrament, just gazing in loving adoration in times of silent prayer.

I attribute my great longing for this mysterious presence to the presence of the risen Lord in the eucharist. From this "felt" presence I was led to also find him at other times and places: eventually in others and, lo and behold, even in myself.

His real presence in nature, too, always drew me to his silent yet pervasive presence everywhere, with the sacramental presence highlighting it and localizing it in a focused, personal way.

A Long, Difficult Journey

Meditation has been a long, difficult journey all my life, but one that draws me on inexorably. There were times when meditation seemed nothing but an agony to be endured. Times when, maybe because of a lack of right guidance and direction, anxieties and fears and scruples and various emotions would rise and almost swamp my little boat of faith and love. Enlightened guidance is absolutely essential on this journey of meditation.

Ever since I read *The Way of a Pilgrim* some 25 years ago, "The Jesus Prayer" has been a constant companion on my journey, either the full or shortened versions. I have gradually learned to let different mantras arise and unfold over the years, letting them simply and gradually just be there. I have let a word or short phrase such as "Jesus, Abba" become, with constant repetition, just background music, rising and falling as is needed to help focus my mind and heart on God, as distractions inevitably keep rearing their heads.

As the years rolled on I learned more about body posture and breathing. I know these, too, can become prayer, so that I can meditate using the prayer-of-the-body and the prayer-of-the-breath.

Posture, Breath and Silent Awareness

These, coupled with the repetition of the sacred word or mantra, lead to stillness and awareness: awareness of the mystery we call God. Meditation, I now find, is an interplay of these different components: posture, breath, mantra, silent awareness. I find the mantra is always there, ready to be used to still the mind. But there are times when I just can't repeat the mantra, so breath awareness is needed. This is sufficient to still my mind and keep me focused and intent on beating away at the "cloud of unknowing," and frees me from becoming entangled in the stream of distractions when they arise. I have found different methods helpful, but only if I use them as aids to prayerful union with God in love and faith, rather than as ends in themselves.

The Influence of Bede Griffiths

Then, in 1992, I spent five weeks with Bede Griffiths at Shantivanam in India. Although I had met him in Australia in the late 1980s and had heard him speak of John Main and the Christian Meditation community, it was only there at Shantivanam that I began reading John Main's *Word into Silence*. This book and my conversations with Laurence Freeman coupled with Bede's endorsement of John Main as the foremost contemporary international teacher of Christian Meditation led me to enter into a close association and collaboration with the Christian Meditation community.

The Bridge to Other Religious Traditions

Subsequently, John Main's writings and tapes and Laurence Freeman's retreats and regular excellent articles in the newsletter have brought me into a deep sharing with many meditators on retreats, at conferences and in local groups. John Main's vision, openness and urgent initiative are an inspiration to me and many others in the endeavour to lead people to appropriate the fruits of our Christian contemplative tradition. His vision also throws a bridge across the silence that unites us to other religious traditions in the search for transcendence and spiritual truth.

Meditation practice and its contemplative flowering are for me the very breath and meaning of my life. Without them I would feel empty and lost. For many meditators there are periods, sometimes long or sometimes short, when meditation is abandoned or neglected. It's in these times that one can sense the emptiness in one's daily life. God himself draws us back to the daily discipline.

I have found meditation gives a sense of inner continuity in my life. It helps to connect my inner and outer daily life. It's not a place of escape, but rather a place to encounter yourself at the deepest levels and there to find God and others, too!

Henri Tardy

Fr. Henri Tardy is a member of the religious congregation Oblates of Mary Immaculate (OMI). Born in France, he joined the French Oblates and in 1947 was assigned to Canada's far North, the Mackenzie Vicariate and a parish on Holman Island. After 35 years spent on Holman Island he retired to a hermitage in Kairos House in Spokane, Washington, USA. Then, attracted more and more to a life of deeper solitude, he went to India for three years and joined Jeevan Dhara Ashram in the Himalayas. He now leads a hermit's life and meditates three times daily at an Oblate Retirees House in Edmonton, Alberta, Canada.

My life experience has been one of silence. This is not intended as humour! The world of silence which I call "being on the silence frequency" is a world that is little known and explored, perhaps even by those who are deaf and mute. Real silence resides within.

When I was young, I was attracted by deserts, oceans, high mountains or any region that rests in silence. At the age of 19, I had read only three books other than my school books. They were those of Alain Gerbault, a solitary sailor who had travelled around the world on a little schooner. I dislike books which require 200 pages to say what can be said in 10.

As far back as I can remember, I have always wanted to be a sailor. God and the war guided me elsewhere: to the priesthood. This was ironic because I had always kept my distance from priests! I chose the congregation of the Oblates of Mary Immaculate because they worked as missionaries in the Canadian Arctic. I must admit my choice was also driven by a spirit of adventure and solitude. By the grace of God, I was sent to Holman, the northernmost mission in the Canadian high Arctic. With a little theological baggage and a will to convert the world, I soon found out that I was like a soldier who had no weapons to face the enemy.

The Silence of the Snow-covered Land

My tiny congregation was only three families. My ministry consisted of visiting the families, nursing the sick and managing an arts and crafts cooperative. I spent years looking at the frozen ocean as far as the eye could see, listening to the silence of the snow-covered land and the wind which so often forces you to stay home. I observed the Inuit hunter, who remains motionless for hours, waiting for a seal to harpoon. I observed the silent Inuit traveller riding on his dogsled or building an igloo to shelter from the storm. The whole lifestyle plunged me into the world of silence.

Many years later, I came to meditation. It happened when a young tourist came to take refuge at the mission and spoke to me one evening about contemplative prayer. Slowly I was drawn deeper into the world of silence. It fascinated me, like a cave hunter who slips through narrow passageways with the dim light of a lamp. The lamp I used was not one of knowledge but one of *being*, which is the *heart*, where God dwells. From that moment on, I began to discipline myself and meditated each day, several times a day.

God in the Beauty of a Tiny Flower

After spending 35 years in the arctic, I left because of health reasons. God led me to Kairos, a house of prayer in the United States, where I lived for a number of years in semi-solitude in a hermitage in the woods. I no longer could see the great expanse of desert and space of the arctic. I had to learn to discover God in the beauty of a tiny flower, the comings and goings of small insects, to caress the bark of a tree and identify with these small things of God's creation.

Through a series of events, God led me to other adventures and India. India was like entering a large cave where one discovers paintings thousands of years old. There, I lived in a little ashram, 2000 metres up on the slopes of the Himalayas. I did not try to explore the Indian traditions, for they seemed too complex for my

Western mind. However, I learned to simply let myself soak in the milieu in which I lived as by osmosis.

Everything Speaks of God

Nature was grandiose: the high peaks of the Himalayas, nights filled with stars, a brilliant sun which seems to come out of the mountains. Everything speaks of God. His presence is everywhere and bears names of divinities. Everything becomes one, everything is spiritual and a non-duality. The Western mind may find this concept difficult to understand, but the Eastern contemplative is very much at ease in this world. This experience transformed my life and simplified it. Meditation became a source of replenishment. I began to see my ego, my little self, as something which hindered the manifestation of God. To be freed of the false self, with God's help of course, is to give God free rein so that he may transform my thoughts, words, actions, even my presence into an expression of the divine.

God's Unique Gift: The Present Moment

God does not need words or pictures to express himself. His presence is in itself creative. This gives me great joy because, as the years go by, I have experienced physical and mental limitations. When choosing to live a life of silence and solitude, at times I have felt selfish, or like a parasite removed from the world. However, I began to realize that at the centre of my being, I am at the centre of all creation. In God I am one with my brothers and sisters throughout the world. In God I carry peace, strength and discernment. To those whose vocation is the contemplative life, to be in God is to live in the *present* moment. God's unique gift is this *present moment*, the sole reality of our world.

I have been more talkative than I expected! I have let my pen run. Writing this has, however, given me the opportunity to thank God for his faithful and loving presence throughout my life. Words and thoughts are not important.

Each day, I realize more and more that I am on the fringe of the world of silence just waiting to penetrate it even more. It has become a source of pure joy.

Now that I have aged, my physical and mental faculties are disappearing one after the other. Each "letting go," though, opens a door to the world of silence where the absolute resides, to the world of God which will never end. May your joy and mine be one as I say "Thank you" to the one who *is*.

Seraphim Thomas

Fr. Thomas Paul Hicks, who is known by his religious name, Fr. Seraphim Thomas, lives in Louisville, Kentucky, USA. He is an Anglo-Catholic priest and an hesychast (from the Greek "hesychia," meaning "inner tranquility and calm") living in what he calls a House of Nazareth. Here he lives the spiritual life of ceaseless prayer. He is also founder in formation of the Order of Jesus of Nazareth – OJN. His connection with Christian Meditation led to several visits to John Main's Benedictine Priory in Montreal, Canada.

My first encounter with meditation came in the 1960s through Transcendental Meditation (TM). This was fine for a while, but it always left me feeling there was something more. So I took the usual routes of studying Hinduism and Buddhism and found the same result. Then one day, as I was driving north to a hermitage, it all came in a flash of light. All these techniques and philosophies served only to help me enter into *myself*, and hence I was left wanting more. It was all so simple, I had missed it. For the Christian, the practice of meditation roots us in God because for us this is our ultimate reality.

The practice and the meaning of Christian Meditation for me can all be summed up in a story.

Travel to India

Coffee spilled into my lap as I heard, "Oh! I'm sorry, please forgive me." Grabbing a napkin, I assured the person who had bumped into me that it was okay. As I refilled my cup, I was reminded of a day on a dusty street in New Delhi, India, and how I learned one of the great spiritual lessons of my life.

Some years ago, I travelled to the Jeevan Dhara Ashram located in the foothills of the Himalayan Mountains. I went to pray, meditate and spend time with Sr. Vandana Mataji, who is head of the ashram. My cell looked out on majestic peaks which were breathtakingly beautiful. The air was fresh and scented with mountain flowers; it was a truly idyllic setting. Each morning I would rise at 3 AM to pray the Divine Office and meditate as the sun ignited those majestic peaks with heavenly golden light.

Sr. Vandana's Teaching

Then, with Jesus beads in my hands, I would take a prayer walk which would eventually lead me to the chapel of the Ashram where we would meditate as a community. The meditation would "end" with Vandana sounding the temple bell and telling us to prepare very, very slowly to come out of meditation.

She reminded us that if at this moment your mind and heart are calm, then let that peace which is the presence of God move slowly to the surface of consciousness. If you have entered into stillness, you will need to move to the "surface" of your consciousness very slowly and gently. If your mind is agitated and restless at this moment, take two or three deep breaths, centre yourself and obtain at least surface peace. Now, let your mind bring before you anyone in your life with whom your heart is not at peace, any situation in which there is conflict and let the peace our Lord has given you in your meditation move out from you to that person or situation. You do not have to create the peace, it is already there to be given to those most in need. Now we send it out into the world symbolically by chanting "Om Shanti" three times. Keeping your eyes closed, bow in a gesture of adoration to the presence of God within and around you. Only when you're ready should you begin to open your eyes and welcome the environment around you. Such was Vandana's teaching at the end of meditation.

My days in that mountain paradise seemed to blend into one continuous meditation of bliss. One day I was talking to a pilgrim who had just arrived from Germany. As we discussed the beauty and calm of the ashram I said, "It sure is easy to be holy in a place like this," and he said, "Ya, it sure is," as we gazed on the valley below.

New Delhi and the Jesus Prayer

A week later I made my way to New Delhi, where I spent my days walking the streets, silently saying the Jesus Prayer. I was still swimming in the holiness of the ashram when a motorized rickshaw ran up on the walk, heading straight for me! As the driver was bearing down on me I thought, surely he wouldn't hit me on purpose! How wrong I was – I bounced off the front of the rickshaw. I landed on the ground and yelled, "You idiot!" as he drove off waving his arms and blowing his horn. Dusting myself off I said, "Oh well, forget it," and walked on, keeping a careful eye open for ricks.

The Test of Holiness Is in the Marketplace

Suddenly the noise of the city faded entirely as my thoughts turned inward to that space where God speaks to us beyond words and images. A week before I had been in a Himalayan bliss, so "close" to God, so spiritual and saying, "It's easy to be holy in a place like this." Now, the first time I'm with someone since then I get angry and call him an idiot! I suddenly realized it's easy to *think* you can be holy in a place like an ashram. The test of holiness, however, is not being in an ashram, on a mountain, or in one's set times of meditation. The real test is carried out in the marketplace where life bumps us literally and figuratively.

Back in the present, as I took another sip of coffee, I thought, the reason coffee was spilled on me was not because I was accidentally bumped but because there was coffee in the cup to begin with. What's inside a person is what comes out when they are bumped. We are to be filled with Christ so that when we are bumped, out come forgiveness, understanding, encouragement, compassion, love, and whatever the present moment demands.

David Wood

David Wood, a retired Anglican priest, lives with his wife, Sheila, in Maryport, in Cumbria, the Lake District of England. He is the Christian Meditation coordinator in this area of the country and he and Sheila regularly visit meditation groups and organize speaking functions on the topic of contemplative prayer. They are both hikers and climb the "fells" in this beautiful part of England.

I discover I am in good company with Bede Griffiths, the Benedictine monk who lived the last 45 years of his long life at the heart of a Christian ashram in India. Before he went there he tells how he spent 17 thriving years at Prinknash Abbey in England where, day after day, he and his companions spent extensive times together in silent prayer. "But," he said, "no one had ever taught us *how* to use the silence." There was simply no explanation at that time of how to pray contemplatively.

So it was with me. For years I searched for a way to pray in silence. I knew in my heart how important it was. I was an ordained Anglican priest. I trained counsellors in the art of being still and silent and listening. I developed weeklong prayer workshops on one of Britain's most sacred islands, at Lindisfarne, where St. Aidan brought Christianity to Britain in 635 A.D. Silence was a large part of these times: whole days of silence in such a place! I pursued a sabbatical journey for three months, staying in contemplative communities in France, Belgium and Germany. I spent Holy Week in a deep silent retreat at Taizé as thousands and thousands of young people gathered for Easter. But through all of this I never found a "way."

It all had its place and its time. In reality, though, I became more confused, for at the same time my personal life disintegrated and my marriage ended. Yet two heartbeats throbbed away persistently in my centre and would not be silenced: *community* and *silence*. This was my direction, my beckoning. I held on to them. Or perhaps they held on to me.

I Knew that I Was Home

I embarked on a new marriage in 1988, still working in a parish. Then, one evening in November, we went to a meeting called by the Cumbria Fellowship of Contemplative Prayer at the Community of the Holy Name, a women's order in Keswick, Cumbria. An ancient, wrinkled, frail-looking nun with merry eyes and a spirit as large as the winds which sweep our hills read a few words from one of John Main's books. I knew then that I was home. My wife and I both knew simultaneously that here was the pearl of great price. Here was the treasure hidden in the field that I had been looking for all this time.

On Sharing the Gift

This teaching of silence and stillness is what I have wanted to share ever since with whoever is ready to hear that there is a simple way home, to the centre. So many people have been waiting for years and years, feeding only on crumbs with amazing faithfulness. The hunger and thirst for a path of silent prayer is everywhere.

One of the most profound contemporary British poets, R.S. Thomas, cheers us on our way.

> He is that great void
> we must enter, calling
> to one another on our way
> in the direction from which
> he blows. What matter

if we should never arrive
to breed or to winter
in the climate of our conception?
Enough we have been given wings
and a needle in the mind
to respond to his bleak north.
There are times even at the Pole
when he, too, pauses in his withdrawal
so that it is light there all night long.

I think that maybe
I will be a little surer
of being a little nearer.
That's all. Eternity
is in the understanding
that the little is more than enough.

Chapter 7

Meditation, Aging, Illness and Death

"Hitting Rock Bottom"

Joyce Donoghue
Al of Hobart
Nancy Kadrovach
David A. Kruse
Mary Orth-Pallavicini
Carol McDonough
Bonye Norton
Antoinette O'Reilly
Katharine Thomas
Donna Wojtyna
Sheila Wood
Serena Woon

Joyce Donoghue

Joyce Donoghue is an Anglican with five children and five grandchildren who lives in West Sussex, England. She has been a civil servant, magazine columnist and editor of a community newspaper and has published both poetry and children's books. For eight years she was a training and development officer for a voluntary organization. Joyce started a Christian Meditation group in 1995.

Like John Main, I was a wartime teenager. Unlike Fr. John, I was brought up in the Church of England, though with additional Catholic and Evangelical input: a mixed Christian education! At 18 I went off to try the town's other churches. I recall disliking the prescribed prayers, feeling they should be *extempore,* or at any rate personally composed, and finally joined what is today the United Reformed Church (URC). I am now a member of our local Anglican church.

On January 8, 1994, I read an article in *The Guardian*'s "Face to Faith" column about a monk called Laurence Freeman and his book *A Short Span of Days.* As I read it I knew that this was what I'd been looking for all my life. I grabbed pen and paper and wrote to the London Christian Meditation Centre asking for more information. A week later, on January 15, when the introductory sheet arrived, I began there and then to meditate.

It was soon apparent that I couldn't have chosen a greater challenge. Everyone has trouble with distractions; I was already having increasing difficulty keeping my mind on other forms of communication, so how was I to attempt to keep tuned-in to one word for up to 30 minutes? I plunged in anyway. And as one with a gift for words, always able to spin a pretty prayer, I felt that confining myself to one word seemed an appropriate sacrifice.

Mantra on Automatic Pilot

As the weeks passed, the mantra would sometimes take charge, breaking in, as it were, upon my distractions: mantra on automatic pilot, mind elsewhere! Occasionally, at the very end of a distraction-filled session, it still does so, reassuringly. At other times, meditation moves into a phase of several minutes without distraction, accompanied by an extraordinary sense of love received and given, an enfolding, a resting in the peace of God: perhaps what George Maloney S.J. describes as *enstasis*.

Our Journey Is Not Linear but Spiral

It seems to me that our journey is not linear but spiral, going ever more deeply down to our centre yet, as we go deeper, passing through places we have visited before and seeing them differently. As we walk, limp, stumble on our way, the distractions are still there, and we are increasingly left unaided to discover our own essential weakness, dependency and poverty. Very humbling!

On the path we are, and always will be, beginners, but as we become stronger, more disciplined and committed, we begin, however fleetingly, to enter our "inner chamber" or the "cave of the heart." But not of our own volition: our part is to simply "rest in the Lord and wait patiently for him." In John Main's words, to "stay with the mantra."

On this journey our concern is with the present moment, and the manner of our travelling must be all important. It is not *when* or *how* we shall arrive, for whoever sets out on this journey and keeps with it has in a sense already arrived. Our part is poverty, patience and persistence. And although we take nothing with us, in fact we take everything, for we take our whole selves.

Accepting One's Limitations

Back to everyday practicalities. At the outset I had to decide on time and place and it was soon clear that the only times secure from interruption were early morning and at bedtime. The only place was my bedroom. I tried a chair and tried the floor, neither of which did any good for my back or my legs, which need to be kept up as much as possible. I ended up on my bed, as Bede Griffiths himself preferred in his old age. Whereas I used to read in bed, I now read a few pages of one of the Christian Meditation books and set my stopwatch for meditation. If I do nod off, tomorrow I may be more clear-headed. Nowadays I am a bit dopey in the mornings because of medication, so I have a cup of tea and listen to some of *Today* on the radio before meditating. It's a question of timing and of accepting one's limitations.

Growing older and accepting that there are things one cannot do is part of self-acceptance. I had to give up attending the meditation group only four months after starting it. It had seemed so urgent to make a beginning that summer of 1995. We began in July and in August I fell ill. But the group continues and I see that my part was to get it going. Some plant seeds, some reap.

The Holy Trinity and John Main

Highlights for me as a meditator have been two day retreats at Worth Abbey with Fr. Laurence, whose books and newsletters are my greatest inspiration. I do have several tapes of both John Main and Fr. Laurence, but mostly lend them to others, knowing I concentrate better on the written word. As I work through the Christian Meditation literature in an ever-extending cycle, there is always something new and relevant. I have found the theology of meditation particularly satisfying and have learnt more about the Holy Trinity from John Main than from anyone else.

That these later years should be so filled with spiritual exploration and practice is a wonderful gift, and it is a privilege to be able, so belatedly, to make a useful contribution. By grace, I have been given the time, the route map and an outline of the journey. "My song is love unknown," indeed.

For the individual, meditation is a gift of grace. In a wider context, the challenge for all Christians today is to acknowledge that we are *one* family. Meditation offers both the way and the means to go beyond our denominational differences and thence towards dialogue with the other world faiths.

Al of Hobart

Members of Alcoholics Anonymous value their anonymity highly and so this contribution is by "Al of Hobart," Tasmania, Australia. His hope is that this story will help other people understand better the illnesses of alcoholism and drug addiction and the vital role Christian Meditation can play in the recovery process.

It took a lot of pain and a final "rock bottom" for me to come to my first AA meeting in February 1994. By this time my life had become quite chaotic, and disintegration of body, soul and spirit was well underway.

I had discovered John Main nine years earlier and found that meditation was a form of prayer I had hungered for. For many years I had used alcohol and tranquillizers to help ease the pain of living. They provided a release from the worries and concerns of life and anaesthetized me against reality. As a married person with three children and a challenging career, I found it increasingly difficult to cope without the aid of some chemical. What I didn't know was that I was entering the "fast-track" of alcoholism and drug addiction.

As a young child I grew up in a tense family situation and found it difficult to cope with many of my family's ups and downs. My family arrived in Australia when I was two years old, and we joined the statistics of the post-War migration. This exodus, and the war experiences of my Ukrainian-born dad, placed enormous strains on him which subsequently broke his health. Unfortunately, I became something of a lightning rod for Dad's disenchantment.

Religion and Alcohol as Anaesthesia

Religion provided an anaesthetic from all the pain of that time. I developed a deep faith in Mary and the saints and constantly asked them to intercede for me and my troubled family. To keep my nervousness and anxiety in check, I took up running, relaxation exercises and prayer. The accent was on me "doing" these things to help me to "be" with some degree of comfort. I felt very much out of place in the outer world and lived in an inner world of anxiety and fear.

Thanks to several sympathetic doctors who saw me at that time, I discovered that certain chemicals had properties which would enable me to feel better about myself. They were shock-absorbers against the pain of living. They gave me the serenity to accept the things I could not change. They gave me courage to change the things I could. They even provided the "wisdom" for me to know the difference.

However, one day I discovered that alcohol would enhance the effect of these "wonder drugs" and I continued to use both for many years. My depressions increased and a real sense of futility and despair clouded whatever light on the horizon was left. In fact, I began to slip into a deep and dark hole whose sides were greased with despair.

Word into Silence

John Main appeared at just the right time. I had recently changed jobs and found that alcohol and other chemicals were not quite "strong enough" to sustain me. Vocal prayer was stepped up but it didn't seem to help me with day-to-day life. John Main's *Word into Silence* finally provided the key to a method of prayer which would help to unify the disparate parts of myself that were desperately seeking solace. I bought and read all the other books written by John Main and Laurence Freeman and became something of an authority on Christian Meditation.

I meditated daily for over 10 years and enjoyed many of the benefits of this discipline. It seemed to check the downward spiral of my alcoholism and drug addiction and I "levelled out" as my life became a little more manageable. Through meditation I was unwittingly doing some of the Twelve Steps of Alcoholics Anonymous (AA), which involve a process of "Letting go" and "Letting God." (I had not yet joined AA.)

The Black Hole of the Ego

However, alcohol and drugs continued, from time to time, to feed my ego and distort reality to the degree that I was unaware of how critical my illness was becoming. My life was one of growing isolation, selfishness and a sense of unreality. My ego had become a black hole and I was exiled from my self. I was losing the ability to relate to myself and to other people. Those closest to me lived a life parallel to mine but never intersecting.

But for the grace of God, this state of affairs would have continued towards a miserable end. The very grace that had introduced me to Christian Meditation now introduced me to Alcoholics Anonymous. I now have two "Big Books." The first is the Christian scriptures. The Bible anchors me to my spiritual heritage as a Catholic born and baptized in Germany, with a Ukrainian-rite dad and a Latin-rite mum. The second Big Book is that of AA, which provides a program of living one day at a time. The Twelve Steps are a path to a new way of living and being. They are complemented by my practice of Christian Meditation, which is based on humility and the deflation of the ego so that the self can push through the obstacles of distraction and attachments.

The Source of Healing, Wholeness and Holiness

As a recovering alcoholic and addict, I find that meditation puts me in direct contact with the source of healing. Like the paralytic in the gospel, I need a community of friends to make an opening, remove the tiles of my ego and then help lower me down to Jesus, the source of healing, of wholeness and holiness. I have a crowd of distractions that pushes against me and threatens to overwhelm me. Fear, anger, resentment and despair are just some of this crowd that prevents access to healing. Meditation helps clear the debris and offers the possibility of a grace-filled life. One of the saddest manifestations of alcoholism and drug addiction is the tremendous loss of self-esteem. A life that runs on ego is very shallow indeed; finding wholeness for the victims of this illness is about recovering self-esteem.

Discovering John Main has been a resurrection experience. However, there is no resurrection without a Holy Thursday and a Good Friday. I have meditated through the paschal cycle and have experienced the bitter and sweet seasons of life. The Spirit of Jesus has called me to a new way of life, which is one of love and faithful service: a life that is in relationship with self, others and God.

Thanks to John Main and the founders of Alcoholics Anonymous, I now have solace in the midst of storms. Jesus' words on the Lake of Galilee ring out: *"Peace, be still!"* (Mark 4:39)

Nancy Kadrovach

Nancy Kadrovach is a widow living in the home that she and her husband, Dan, built together in the rolling hills of the Ozarks on Bull Shoals Lake in Arkansas, USA. She gardens extensively, has a small cattle operation, studies ancient Greek and paints botanical watercolours. She is also an oblate of Subiaco Benedictine Abbey in Central Arkansas.

On Friday, April 17, 1998, close friends and family gathered at Arlington National Cemetary near Washington, D.C., to celebrate my husband's life with tears and laughter before as much of him as could die was laid to rest in hallowed ground. Among those who followed the horse-drawn caisson with its flag-draped coffin was our daughter Karen, now terminally ill with the same kind of cancer that took Dan from us.

Let me write of Christian Meditation within the context of loss, hoping that someone who reads it will find reassurance. Anne Morrow Lindbergh said that she didn't believe that suffering by itself made us wise. We all suffer, yet wisdom remains relatively rare. Before we can discover meaning, we must allow time for mourning. Only then can we give sorrow words and try to tell our story. As our Lord promised, we don't face desolation alone. He was with Dan and me to the end of the world as we had known it.

I do not know how to describe Dan's courage and fortitude and faith in his dying, even until the hour of his death. My part during those terrible months was simple, though not always easy. I handled the logistics of his medical treatments, kept family and friends informed about how we were dealing with it, and tried to be present to the grace and joy in the days still left to us. Dan and I were given three more seasons together. Knowing that we did familiar things for the last time was like licking honey off the edge of a knife blade.

On Keeping a Spiritual Journal

I was introduced to Christian Meditation eight years ago by a dear friend from New Orleans. We've meditated together a handful of times, and share books and tapes between visits. Mostly I meditate in solitude. I live in a remote area of the Ozarks and I've not been able to find other people with whom I can pray. When I began the morning and evening spiritual discipline of meditation I retained some of my previous spiritual practices, including keeping a spiritual journal.

A retired sister of the Order of the Sacred Heart had given me the first slender blank notebook more than 10 years ago, with her assurance that I'd be better able to discern God in my life in retrospect. It's been exactly as she said. Journal-keeping has the quality of a conversation with an other that one has loved for a long time, so that words are almost superfluous. <u>Meditation is too elusive to describe, but it seems a little like an electromagnetic signal which I can follow on my true path.</u>

Through the Valley of the Shadow of Death

For the past three years, that path has been through the valley of the shadow of death that the psalmist sang about. My father died on July 23, 1995, in the fullness of his years. Almost immediately thereafter, my fragile 92-year-old mother was hospitalized with what still seems to me to have been a broken heart. Somehow we managed to hold onto her for almost a year, time enough for a peaceful reconciliation to loss. Then my younger brother, Frank Gatlin, died on Holy Thursday, 1996, following a heroic 10-day struggle. As he died, he murmured, "Home, home...." Amen, Frank. Both my father and my brother were graduates of Texas A & M University. At Aggie Muster on April 21, 1996, a ceremony held yearly anywhere in the world that there are Aggies, both their names were on the list of fallen comrades. As the names were read aloud, other Aggies responded, "Present." For me, they will always be thus.

One Day at a Time

It is well that we don't know what lies ahead. I don't think I could have held my ground these past three years other than one day at a time. Mother's death and Dan's cancer diagnosis came simultaneously. Through the losses, each different, my twice-daily practice of meditation continued essentially unchanged. I don't remember ever praying for a miracle. The mantra simply began saying itself continuously and spontaneously, resonating in my waking and my sleeping life within an infusion of energy and strength which I shall never understand. God's sufficient grace was just there for both of us. When we reached the limits of what medicine could do, we knew that we wanted Dan to die at home. Dan's internist was supportive, even though he was a hundred miles away. Family was much farther. I had no experience with death's realities and no practical nursing skills, and I didn't know how I was going to manage, but I never doubted that all would be well.

Freed from the Fear of Death

Dan died on Sunday, May 11, 1997, in his own bed, surrounded by our love and our prayers. So luminous was the manner of his passage that those of us who were with him have been freed from the fear of death. I stand now at the end of the beginning, still strengthened and comforted by the mantra. What will happen to our brave and beautiful Karen, with six children who need her? None of this can I understand, but my heart reaches out to whoever reads these words with the promise that I know for myself that all manner of things will be well.

David A. Kruse

David A. Kruse is an attorney-at-law and senior partner in Kruse and Kruse, attorneys in Auburn, Indiana, USA. He married his wife, Pat, in 1966 and they have one son, Andrew Kruse, who is attending law school. He is a member of the Board of Directors for Legal Services, a corporation which provides legal services to the poor, and a member of the Indiana State Bar Association, the American Bar Association and the Trial Lawyers Association.

I have a spinal condition which requires me to lie face down under a "Baker's Oven" for about 20 minutes each morning. Following that, my wife, Pat, gives me a rub-down, and I then do some routine exercises to get my body ready for the day. I used to listen to the radio on the way to work. Now, I find myself frequently leaving the radio off and repeating "*Maranatha*" as a way of preparing my spirit for the oncoming day. This is simply a way of opening my heart and life to God's working in the present moment of this day. At this juncture in my journey, I feel I am "on the way." I am far from consistent, but I feel invited to continue on the path.

Meditating Flat on One's Back

I am an attorney and because of court hearings, I cannot always get time for this way of prayer at midday. But frequently I do get time three days a week and sometimes every day for meditation. We have a separate storage room at home with a couch where I can get away for my daily prayer time. I usually read some devotional literature, then try to follow a pattern of a prayer of thanksgiving, prayer for selected others, and then prayer asking for God's personal guidance and strength. Then I sometimes recite from memory some scripture, such as the Twenty-third Psalm or the Lord's Prayer. I then turn to the "Jesus Prayer" and now the *Maranatha* prayer. I try to enter into a stillness and an awareness of God's abiding presence. I need to lie flat on my back for a portion of this time because of my physical limitations. I frequently enter into a resting time of stillness in which I feel I have surrendered into the love of God. Again, I feel a beginner, just at the threshold. The divine presence, though, invites me to come further.

C.S. Lewis Helpful in the Journey

I first heard of John Main through the publication *Schola Contemplationis*, edited by Beatrice Bruteau and James Somerville. I also first heard of Bede Griffiths through *Schola Contemplationis*, which I started reading in 1984. I have since learned in reading this publication that C.S. Lewis knew Bede Griffiths and that they corresponded. This is interesting to me because C.S. Lewis's book *Mere Christianity* was valuable in my journey through the skepticism of my early college years, about 30 years ago. G.K. Chesterton and Francis Schaeffer were two other authors who helped me see that as Christians we can know there are good and sufficient reasons for believing that God exists and that he has spoken to us in his Son Jesus Christ and in his revealed written word.

From the Head to the Heart

As important as "head knowledge" is, the heart is even more important. We need to enter into the daily experience of *"the mystery* kept hidden from the ages but revealed to our day and time." I believe as I was taught, that the mystery is *"Christ in you, the hope of glory."* (Colossians 1:26-27) John Main's meditation teaching gives us a tool within our Christian tradition to make that mystery a living reality. I am motivated by this truth to continue seeking an ever-increasing awareness of God's presence and spirit.

What appeals to me in John Main's *Essential Teaching* tapes on meditation is that he presents meditation within the context of the truth of traditional Christian teaching. He does not see meditation as isolated from the gospel, but rather as the *experiential* fulfillment of the gospel. Christ promised to send the Comforter, the Spirit of Truth, to dwell within us. We are one of the many mansions in the Father's house within which he dwells. (John 14)

But we are so often busy with other things that we forget about the moment-by-moment, abiding presence of God. John Main encourages a prayer whose meaning is fully consistent with orthodox Christianity: "*Maranatha*," "Our Lord Comes" or "Come, Lord Jesus." (1 Corinthians 16:22) In this prayer, we leave our business activities behind and open ourselves to stillness and the presence of God within us in our daily times of prayer.

My wife, Pat, my son, Andrew, and I attend the Church of God, where Pat is the church librarian. Andrew is a spiritually sensitive young man who has just graduated from college and is headed to law school. He seeks to serve God by helping the cause of justice in our world. We are grateful for the rich heritage of spiritual treasures the Catholic Church and monastic tradition have preserved and made available to all who are seekers.

Mary Orth-Pallavicini

Mary Orth-Pallavicini lives in New York City. After her six children were grown, she went back to school and graduated from Fordham University. She then got her Master's of Divinity at Union Theological Seminary. Mary worked on a chaplaincy team at Lenox Hill Hospital for six years and retired soon after her husband died. She facilitates a meditation group at Holy Family Church in New York City.

Very soon after I became a Catholic 50 years ago I felt drawn to wordless prayer, but the only help I could find was in books such as *The Cloud of Unknowing*, the works of St. John of the Cross, and Dom Chapman's *Spiritual Letters*. Unfortunately, I got so wound up in trying to find out if I ought to be praying this way that my time became wholly taken up with *myself*. I muddled along, however, and a little over 20 years ago went to a contemplative monastery in upstate New York for three weeks in search of a deeper prayer experience.

The community used the "Jesus Prayer" from the Eastern Orthodox tradition: "Lord Jesus Christ, Son of God, have mercy on me, a sinner," which they shortened to "Jesus, mercy." They had several 40-minute periods a day of silent prayer, each using "Jesus, mercy" as a mantra; they did yoga exercises in the morning as well. I believe with all my heart that by using the short phrase or mantra to lead us into the deep silence, we come into the healing presence of the spirit of Christ. The days were spent in silence, reading, cooking, weeding in the vegetable garden and cleaning up.

I loved being there, but when I returned to my husband and six children in New York, I found it very hard to find the time to meditate. I did the best I could. Several years later I had the joy of finding Dom John Main's book *Word into Silence*. For the first time I felt I was on the right path and that all things are possible in faith, even finding silence in a large family! I did have to learn to get up earlier in the morning, though.

Joys as Well as Sad Times

I had no idea of the vast changes in my life that lay ahead of me. First, I went back to college. I had only had one year of college before my marriage, and when I returned to college my professors suggested that I go on to a seminary. I did this, getting my Master's of Divinity at Union Theological and later serving on a Catholic chaplaincy team at Lenox Hill Hospital for six years.

Then my husband was diagnosed with a terminal illness. I left my job to take care of him with the wonderful help of the Visiting Nurses Association Hospice. This was an extremely difficult time and I never would have been able to see it through without my daily meditation.

I have known tremendous joys as well as sad times and have made wonderful new friends within the meditating community.

Among the great gifts that meditation brings is the development of friendships among those who meditate together. Five years ago I started to facilitate a group at Holy Family Church in New York.

There for Each Other in Times of Crises

The group meetings are an oasis in our lives, giving us the refreshment of renewed courage and hope. Over time we can see our commitment deepening and our understanding growing. We are there for each other in all sorts of crises, and have all noted that we go into a deeper meditation when we are meditating together. We all find that our twice-daily practice is a source of strength, healing and continual growth. In our weekly group sessions we listen to a tape of Fr. Main or Fr. Laurence, meditate for half an hour and then listen to a short reading and discuss whatever is on our minds.

I am struggling now with a painful illness which doctors can't seem to treat, but I am held up and kept going by my two periods of meditation. My heart is at peace because I know I am on my own true path no matter what difficulties turn up. Most of my children are now practising some form of meditation, which is a great joy for me.

I pray that our community will grow with the passing of each year and help to bring peace to our world.

Carol McDonough

Carol McDonough lives in the Ca-naan Network Community on the Mornington Peninsula, south of Melbourne, Australia. She was led to meditation through John Main's book Word into Silence *and started several meditation groups in Bendigo, Victoria. She has been involved in the Peninsular spirituality network, which distributes information about the teaching of Christian Meditation and the location of meditation groups. This story was told to Vicki Renner, a friend of Carol's.*

I think I've been meditating and seeking God in stillness since I was a child but didn't have a label or word for it. There are three specific happenings I remember. As a child in the 1950s and 1960s I would climb a banksia tree in Tootgarook on the Mornington Peninsula (southwest of Melbourne) every summer holiday. In the top of this tree I would sit and in a childlike way meditate in silence along with the tree.

I lived in the inner city of Melbourne and I used to sit above the creek near my house and make little houses out of aniseed. This for me was an act of worship though I didn't name it that at the time. And at the Methodist church I sat and stared at the text up at the front, which said: "I worship the Lord in the beauty of holiness." I used to go into what I can now name as a still, centred place. When I was older, in my late teens and early 20s, I became a mountaineer. Sitting on top of mountains after a hard climb had the same spiritual effect as climbing the banksia tree, making aniseed houses and meditating on the church text.

From 1968 to 1981 were the years of marriage, career, travelling and trying to have babies. I still used to take time out to sit and be quiet but it was not my top priority. Then in 1980 and 1981 two of my babies died, Donald of Sudden Infant Death Syndrome at 11 weeks, and Emma after a premature labour.

Hitting Rock Bottom

In the devastation of Donald's death, there was one glimmer of light. I can remember a few days after he died that I was whimpering and feeling as if I was being held. I sensed love and compassion flowing from other people into my pain. That feeling stayed with me through the ensuing months of hell. But all of that love and compassion deserted me when my daughter, Emma, died. Still believing I'd suffocated Donald, and having now lost Emma, I hit rock bottom.

One week later, I stood looking out a picture window at the magnificent landscape garden in the hills where I lived. I decided then that I would continue to live. The earth seemed too beautiful to leave. The next morning at dawn I went into Sherbrooke Forest (a local national park) and found a huge eucalyptus regnans, or mountain ash, the tallest hardwood tree on earth, and sat with my back to its trunk, supported by its roots. I went through what can only be described as an adult mystical experience. Only looking back do I have a framework to name it.

A Sense of Being Held

I had a real sense, again, of being held. I had a sense of the slow heartbeat of the Earth, a sense of the long, slow growing of the tree, its mulch at its feet. I had a sense of the whole cycle of life and death, which renews life, and the oneness of all creation. And I knew the children were all right. I'd never consciously known that, but I think I'd always known it at a deeper level. And I knew that in spite of the utter, wrenching loss, somehow it would be possible to go on – not easy, but possible.

The next couple of years I hung on. The marriage was over. They were very dark years. Life was difficult but the glimmers of light in the trees kept me going. Paradoxically, living on the earth got harder as the trauma of those years severely aggravated my undiagnosed chemical and radiation sensitivities.

Starting a Jacob's Wrestling Match

By 1982 I had got to the point of saying, "If there is a God, then a God that removes children is worse than Hitler and I'm not interested. In fact, I'm more consumed with rage than I can say." But looking back, I can see I'd started my own Jacob's wrestling.

One day I wandered into a bookshop called The Word of Life. Two books jumped off the shelves at me. One was *Beginning to Pray* by Antony Bloom, which talks of being taken to rock bottom and being given hope on the other side of despair. That was exactly my experience. Hope grew and despair withered.

I also picked up *Word into Silence,* by John Main. I devoured it at home because it was naming my spiritual and suffering experiences in language that had integrity and authenticity for me. The book enabled me to reclaim in new and adult language the mystical Christianity of my childhood.

Into the Deep, Wordless Silence

In the back of the book there was information about the Christian Meditation Network in Montreal and in the front, brief instructions on how to meditate. Apart from the mantra, *Maranatha,* this meditation was really a reminder of my childhood searching for inner stillness. I was already into this deep wordless silence. The book gave me the courage to take meditation into my workplace, which at that stage was the Uniting Church Prahran Mission.

The mission welcomed into its community the poorest of the poor. They were people with multiple disabilities (physical, intellectual and psychiatric) living in supported accommodation. Whoever turned up on any particular morning, clients and staff alike, would spend 20 minutes in meditation together. It created a wonderful sense that we were a community, living and working together, and that the mission was a good place to be. It changed the sense of the place from "staff" and "clients" to "we together." Meditation created community.

After some time travelling in Europe, my health deteriorated dramatically. In early 1985 I was finally diagnosed as having multiple chemical and radiation sensitivities. I was told that I had only months to live. As I lay in bed racked with pain, I was given yet another gift. I felt I was taken beyond the physical pain into the timeless, pain-free space of oneness. For months I was on oxygen around the clock to keep me alive. I used to lie in the dark or in the day waiting for the gift of stillness which was my only relief, as I was unable to take painkillers.

Starting Two Meditation Groups

At last I realized that my only chance of survival was to get out of the smog of Melbourne. So I shifted to Bendigo, in county Victoria, where I improved enough to go off oxygen. I joined the Anglican Cathedral Choir and met Diana, who was also a member of the prayer and worship committee. In Lent 1985 Diana and the Dean of the Cathedral led a four-day program of forms of prayer. At my suggestion, one session was on Christian Meditation, based on John Main's teaching. After Lent, Diana and I asked if we could form a Christian Meditation group at the Cathedral. We discovered there was a Christian Meditation Network in Australia and started two groups, which flourished.

In 1988, we decided to run a public "What is meditation?" day at the local community centre. We learned a big lesson. We decided we'd pray "Lord, bring the people you want" and we put out chairs for 20. Ninety-two people packed into the room, partly to hear John Main! (The local paper in error had advertised that he would be speaking.) We're sure he was with us in spirit and enjoying the humour of the situation. Three more groups formed as a result of this day, one of which met at my home for three years.

Survival in Quietness

By 1992 my health had deteriorated seriously and I was on oxygen again for the whole year. I discovered the only place I could survive was at the beach. So I shifted to the Mornington Peninsula, south of Melbourne. I spent my first two-and-a-half years on the peninsula being very quiet, trying to get well. Three years ago I moved to the place I live now, three-and-a-half acres of coastal bushland called Ca-naan Network Community.

Together with the Spirituality Network, we turned 1998 into a year of pilgrimage. We advertised Ca-naan as one of the resting places on an eight-day meditative walk.

Those who live here meditate together in their own way in the various gardens, including the labyrinth, the bush sanctuary, the permaculture food gardens, and the Mary garden, with its gentle succulents. The spirit of meditation is expressed in our daily lives as we work, eat, cook, walk and tend the gardens.

Bonye Norton

Bonye Norton studied at Eversholme International School, Florence, Italy, and graduated from Connecticut College, New London, CT, USA, with a BA in philosophy. She has been a full-time mother and homemaker in Baltimore, Maryland, with three children: Charles (born in 1962 and killed in 1990 at age 27), Robin and Leslie. Her husband is an Episcopal priest who has taught college philosophy and philosophical theology.

Our lives are a tapestry of all the people and experiences affecting it. The tapestry of my life was deeply rent when our elder son was killed in a bicycle accident in February 1990. I have been able to bind the edges of the hole to prevent further unravelling, but no amount of invisible weaving can repair the damage. In time, the hole fills with cobwebs and it is not so noticeable until something knocks into the web and rips it momentarily. The cobwebs, however, quickly grow back.

Meditation had prepared me for this loss and has carried me through it. Despite tremendous support from family and friends, the loss would have been much more difficult to accept without the deep faith, that gift of grace, which meditation has given me. While we have grieved for ourselves, we have never been in mourning for Charles. We knew he was all right. While we were sorrowing, we still experienced joy and, most important of all, peace. We asked *how* this could have happened to an experienced racer but we never once had to ask *why* it happened.

The Death of a Child

I am a talker and acknowledge that I know what I'm thinking when I hear it said aloud. My husband is a thinker. In talking and talking and talking after Charles' death, Howard and I came up with this metaphor: When an artist completes a work of art, he or she cannot add another stroke without compromising the work; when a composer finishes a symphony, no matter how beautiful, he or she cannot add another note without violating the integrity of the work. Evidently Charles, at 27, had completed his purpose in this world, and to have added quantity would have compromised the quality of his life.

Mother Catherine Grace, at All Saints Convent, Catonsville, had taught meditation to a group of clergy spouses four years before Charles' death. Our group had asked her for spiritual guidance in dealing with stress and this led to the practice of meditation. We were so thirsty for this gift that we continued to meet once a month at the convent to meditate for the next 10 years. It has changed our lives.

"A Remarkable Change in Myself"

I soon saw remarkable changes in myself when I disciplined my life to meditating twice a day. Meditating once a day did not work at all. Then my husband saw such a change in me that he looked into it, read much of John Main's material to make sure it was theologically sound, and began meditating with me. I am sure that the fact that we do it together has made it easier to stick to the discipline. We are now two people who are more centred and who share a greatly strengthened faith.

Antoinette O'Reilly

Antoinette O'Reilly lives in Naas, County Kildare, Ireland. She spent two years in New York City with her husband, Peter, a broadcaster and journalist who worked with the United Nations before his death in 1995. A graduate in Montessori studies, Antoinette has worked in various capacities, including six years in a Dublin centre for people with mental hand-

icaps. *For the past 10 years she has been working with the local County Kildare branch of the Dyslexia Association. She has recently completed a book on her late husband's life based on his papers and memorabilia.*

When I began to write this piece, I started to glimpse a series of steps on my spiritual journey. On reflection, I realized that all of them took place at precisely the right time in my life.

About 15 years ago, I was recovering from a serious illness and was feeling rather depressed as a consequence. Several of my friends were practising Transcendental Meditation (TM) and suggested that I try it, which I did. So for some time afterwards, I meditated twice a day, using the "meaningless mantra" I had been given. Looking back, I think it was quite a good preparation for what was to come, although a feeling of dissatisfaction was beginning to creep in. Why was this, I wondered?

Introduction to John Main's Writings

I was fortunate to have a very wise friend, Anne, who was further along the road than I was. She, too, had practised TM but was now a Christian meditator and leader of a small group. She introduced me to John Main's writings and I took a cautious step under her guidance. The idea of silent prayer had always appealed to me, but to realize now that such prayer had deep Christian roots gave me great joy.

Then, for family reasons, my husband and I moved some 20 miles from Dublin to live in County Kildare. Here, unlike in Dublin, there was no meditation group. However, I continued to meditate on my own, and kept in touch with meditators in Dublin.

While serving on the local parish council, I came to know Sr. Catherine, a retired Mercy sister. We would often discuss spiritual matters and, inevitably, the topic of prayer would come up. I told her about John Main and suggested that she might like to come with me to a retreat at the Carmelite Retreat Centre in Dundrum. She quickly agreed.

For several years after that, Sr. Catherine and I meditated together, meeting either in her convent or in my house. This continued until a newly ordained curate, Fr. John Cummins, came to the parish. He organized a series of talks on prayer and asked Sr. Catherine and me to present something on Christian Meditation. Neither of us felt competent to do this so I made a hasty phone call to Dublin for help. An experienced meditator came to our aid and gave an inspiring talk to a small group.

Leading a Group

At the end of the evening, I found that I was now expected to organize and lead a meditation group! Although overwhelmed by feelings of inadequacy, I took the step and arranged a meeting for the following week. A larger than expected crowd turned up and I didn't know whether to be pleased or to panic. Predictably, the size of the group decreased and, as time passed, settled into a core group of about six people, including another Mercy sister, who allows us to gather every week in the school staff room.

Many people have joined us for long or short periods and I now feel that our role as a group is to make people aware of the teaching and hope that it will play an important part in their lives. At the moment, too, our group members are all women, though one or two men have come from time to time. Fr. Cummins is now in Rome and is part of a Christian Meditation group there.

Death of a Husband

For me, there is a sense of "rightness" about it all. Two years ago, after some years of ill health, my husband became seriously ill and was rushed to hospital. It was a Thursday, the day our group usually met. Someone else led the meditation for me so I could be at my husband's bedside. He died during the time of meditation and was doubtless helped by the prayer of my meditating friends. Indeed, they have continued to support me through the time of bereavement.

Now I am hoping to take what may be a final step on the road, that of becoming a Benedictine oblate. During this time of preparation and discernment, I am learning about the Rule of Benedict and the wisdom it has for today's living. I would never have become aware of the richness of the Rule were it not for the influence of meditation and its effect on my life. I am deeply grateful for this and for the friends who have guided me and continue to guide me.

"In the Silence of My Heart, Teach Me Wisdom"

If becoming an oblate is right for me, then it will happen; if not, I will continue to meditate in spite of the "tree full of monkeys" that distracts me from time to time. As the psalmist says, *"In the silence of my heart, teach me wisdom."* (Psalm 51:8) Wisdom is what I continue to seek in my daily meditation.

Katharine Thomas

Katharine Thomas, 34, lives on the edge (as she puts it), in a tiny village on the southern coast of Australia, where the ocean, the Spirit and her health ebb and flow. Living well with chronic illness is a challenge which surpasses her former careers in journalism and corporate communications, and recent training in palliative care counselling. Since 1988, Katharine has led meditation seminars in Adelaide, Sydney, Melbourne, Geelong and Point Lonsdale; edited the Australian Christian Meditation Community newsletter (1993–95); was a member of the national committee; and is a novice oblate of the World Community for Christian Meditation.

Hamlet was right: "To be or not to be" is *the* question which defines our journey. Choosing to *be* more than I *do* is a revolutionary experience. Once, I would have introduced myself by describing what I did for a living. Now, stripped bare of all roles and masks, I say simply where and how I live – on the edge. One day, I hope that I may meet people in a sharing of what truly matters: our states of being beyond boundaries. Yet, describing oneself as "love" and sharing sacred silence is still rather radical! Many meditators understand this urge to be real:

> Meditation is a way of coming to your own centre... to the foundation of your own being, and remaining there... allow[ing] God's mysterious and silent presence within us to become that reality which gives meaning, shape and purpose to everything we do, to everything we are.
>
> (John Main, *Word into Silence*)

Coming to and Remaining at the Centre

Coming to the centre, learning to live less from my unconscious, more aware of the self-conscious, and alive to the supraconscious, has been an extraordinary awakening which I attribute to the purifying process of suffering and the gift of meditation. Becoming Christ-conscious, through sharing the cross and being with God beyond thoughts, words and images, is a profound journey of healing and wholeness, lit by love. There is a gradual fading of self-conscious descriptions of Kate – the little "i," and a deepening sense of God – the big "I."

Ultimately, in moments of exquisite pain and joy, when transient awareness of my body and mind drop away, there is only God, whom the author of *The Cloud of Unknowing* says "is your being and in him you are what you are." Rare as these experiences and insights may be, the effect is enduring. In *Being in Love,* Fr. William Johnston, himself a living flame of love, says that those who are able "to remain at the centre of the soul" dwelling in "loving emptiness, nothingness, silence, and awareness," find their "whole being is unified in love....an unconditional and unrestricted love" which becomes "not just a prayer of being but a prayer of being in love."

On "Being in Love"

"Being in love" is how I experience the deepening practice of Christian meditation. Like all passionate love affairs, my relationship with the Trinity is utterly consuming, requiring total surrender of independence, lifestyle and social securities. Letting go of everything which gives illusory protection – health, relationships, reputation, work, money, possessions – triggers all kinds of spiritual, psychological and physical breakthroughs. Learning to embrace the fear of being alone, misunderstood, rejected, out of control, visibly falling apart and losing the plot, yet trusting that God is with me in this turmoil, is challenging.

Going Over the Edge

Living on and going over the edge is soul-searing stuff. There can be no half-measures, as clinging and bargaining only delay and distort the process of becoming no one and nothing. Mysteriously, that which I dreaded the most, being an *invalid* invalid, has become through grit my saving grace. For it is in the emptying of myself that Christ is filling these spaces with himself, creating new capacities and opportunities for life and service. By rendering me skinless, exquisitely sensitive to joy and suffering, Christ moves in those who are diving deep and surfacing in God. This is the radical transformation described by Fr. Thomas Keating: "once one's being is transformed into Christ, all one's doing becomes anointed with the interior transformation of one's being."

"A Human Being, Not a Human Doing"

My illness and my discovery in meditation that "Kate" was really a human *being,* not a human *doing,* were life-changing turning points which clarified external illusions and interior realities. Striving for success became less important than living a more meaningful, authentic existence. Once I recognized and accepted the transforming power of divine and human love, everything else diminished. Loving God with my whole heart, mind and strength, and loving my neighbour as myself, became greater challenges than scooping the front page of the newspaper and other ephemeral activities.

Crumbling from Within

So how did this urge to be really real evolve? At 16, I started to crumble from within, following a severe infection by the virus known as Epstein-Barr/Mononucleosis/Glandular Fever. Unlike most people, I never recovered, and during the next 17 years my central nervous and immune systems were progressively disabled, damaging my brain, heart, lungs, stomach, bowels, liver, muscles and joints. Paradoxically, this currently incurable, untreatable, chronic and degenerative condition has made me more vulnerable, available and responsive to the Spirit.

Surrendering to the Inner Silence

Since 1988, meditation, spiritual direction, psychotherapy and special friendships have helped in ways that doctors and drugs cannot. In my surrender to the inner silence, stillness and simplicity of meditation, a mysterious process of healing and wholeness is operating in and through my wounded spirit, mind and body. Gently and gradually my fractured sense of separation, of being mortally wounded, is being dissolved through immersion in an infinite sea of love, known to me as God.

Being worn away by the ebb and flow of the Spirit is a humbling experience of increasing awareness and liberation. Unconscious hurts and fears and self-conscious perceptions of pain steadily rise to the surface like bubbles bursting into sea-spray. In the depths beneath the white-capped rips, my heart rests in the swaying seabed where mantra currents ripple, assuring me that real spirituality is not a twice-daily act, but an enduring response to the Spirit in everything, everywhere.

Finding Strength in Weakness

The sea is an apt spiritual metaphor for the journey which anchors me to an ancient peninsula once inhabited by aborigines, convicts and gold-rush pioneers. This vast, jagged shoreline is my cathedral where, strolling from lighthouse to lighthouse and perching on rocks near a cave, I commune with God in creation. Nature and pain have taught me to *be* rather than to *do*, and to find strength in weakness:

> ...what you are is more important than what you do. And this lesson is particularly relevant for the sick, the imprisoned, the aged — for those reduced to inactivity who feel their lives are useless because they are no longer productive... by being they construct a field of energy... [of] wisdom [and]... peace.
>
> (William Johnston, *Being in Love*)

When I am immobilized, only able to be prayed through, the mantra sounds like a fog horn, steering me safely through misty perilous waters into a cove, the cave of the heart. It is there that I offer my whole being, including the broken body, to God. "The praying body is frequently a sick body," says Fr. William Johnston; it is "the weak body of the mystic," "the crucified body of Jesus" and the "elderly" who are "....acutely aware that their being is being-unto-death" (*Being in Love*).

Living on the edge, touching life and death, is a powerful place and state from which to surrender my little self into God's immeasurable self. Simply being still and floating in the sacred silence, inhaling and exhaling the light of Christ, is all it takes to make seemingly purposeless pain infinitely meaningful.

The Experience of "Grace and Grit"

Testifying about the role of meditation in my illness may seem self-absorbed, yet it is precisely the consuming nature of suffering and enlightenment that I am seeking to share with others who are experiencing and supporting such journeys. Enduring, integrating, transcending and sharing the challenges of living and dying is a profound process truthfully described by Ken Wilber as an experience of "grace and grit." He considers transpersonal growth to be something that takes sensitivity, skill and support.

Support is crucial in embarking on spiritual meditation, for without roots in a tradition, a community or a group, a new meditator may be on a potentially perilous path of self-deception. Just as the mantra operates as a fog horn, the meditation group acts as an anchor, stabilizing our tiny vessels in the surging sea of life. Whenever meditators have been beyond their depth, sinking beneath successive changes, losses, griefs, personal breakthroughs and the rigorous stages of meditation, our groups have held hands, becoming buoys for one another.

Most truly, *"where two or three are gathered"* (Matthew 18:20) Christ is there, like a lighthouse beckoning our true selves to emerge from the depths. This is why I believe that the small, hidden, humble meditation group is the visible heart of the ecumenical Christian Meditation community worldwide. For healing and wholeness come from being part of something to which we have made a commitment. In my case, this is the commitment to a cosmic Christ loved in sacred silence with others in a suburban monastery without walls.

The Life-Saving Gift

I am indebted to Pauline Thomas, my beloved mother and pathfinder, who introduced me to Christian Meditation when I was 24 and enthralled by a hedonistic lifestyle that was more self-centred than Christ-centred. Religion seemed dull and irrelevant until Sr. Patricia Sims drew me into a warm circle of meditators. Little did I realize then that meditation would become a life-saving gift on the very eve of my plunge into chaos and the journey beyond.

Donna Wojtyna

Sr. Donna Wojtyna OSB is a member of St. Benedict's Monastery in Pittsburg, Pennsylvania, USA. She leads a Christian Meditation group there of 16 members of whom, as she says, "once in a while all show up." She is also a professional artist who creates basketry and wood sculpture.

My journey into Christian Meditation began in 1988 when, like St. Paul, I was struck from my horse and was invited to focus more on the present moment. Burnout had overtaken me: family caretaking consumed a large amount of my time as well as a very heavy workload. Feeling overextended in almost every facet of my personal and community life, I sought relief in a month's retreat program for religious in Atchison, Kansas. I was only a few months away from celebrating my 25th anniversary in my Benedictine monastery and was searching for something to restore peace and meaning to my world.

Hearing with the Ears of the Heart

The month-long experience in Kansas proved to be the seed of the spiritual renewal for which I yearned. The program offered presenters who shared their insights on the topic of the contemplative in today's world. I found God's special grace for me in the presentation by Fr. Laurence Freeman. I heard with the "ears of my heart" (Rule of St. Benedict) for the first time about Christian Meditation and I felt as if I had been knocked off my high horse! Me – a Benedictine for 25 years and I had never grasped the deep value of this form of prayer! It felt so right! Things were coming together inside of me and I was eager to find the necessary time to sit in silence.

Refreshed, I returned home to Pittsburgh and shared my experience with some of my sisters. Several of them got caught up in my excitement and we decided to meet once a week to practise Christian Meditation. I was happy and satisfied but evidently the Holy Spirit was restless and wanted more.

We Grew, and We Grew, and We Grew

Only a few weeks after our simple but fervent beginnings, a phone call came from a local parishioner. "I am looking for a group that practises contemplative prayer," she said. "Surely the Benedictines must have a group here!" I was concerned that we had so little to offer her as we neophyte meditators were meeting in every nook and cranny of the convent as it was, and struggling with our own meagre attempts to sit in silence. Sensing the Spirit was at work here, and despite some misgivings, I invited Edie to join us. She came and the following week brought two of her friends. We grew, and we grew, and we grew!

Word of mouth has brought those seeking peace to our doorstep and I have been touched and enriched by my fellow travellers. We have a lovely prayer room, simple and perfect for quiet prayer. Adjacent to our prayer space is a small library filled with books and tapes on prayer and contemplation. John Main is no longer a stranger to anyone around here.

At the outset, I was convinced that I was, and continue to be, only an instrument providing a space for Christian Meditation. Since our simple beginnings in 1988, we now have a lovely group of dedicated men and women who faithfully meet once a week for a half hour of shared *Lectio Divina* as well as meditation.

Our First "Daughter" Group

Contemplative prayer is spilling over into our neighbourhood. We have our first "daughter" group: two members from our core group, an Episcopalian minister and one of his parishioners, have extended contemplative prayer to members of their parish. Participants from our group have attended occasionally to support them as they nurture the seed they have planted. We continue to grow. It is an ever-present reminder to me that God is in charge and the Spirit will continue to seek to dwell in open, loving hearts.

I consider it a blessing that I am able to incorporate Christian Meditation into my life's work at the monastery. There I maintain an art studio environment in which I teach and do professional basketry and wood sculpture. At various times throughout the year I provide a day or weekend basketry retreat at the monastery. I also travel to various sites as an invited retreat director, offering spiritual refreshment to small groups in an art-contemplative setting. I have been able to introduce Christian Meditation into the retreat experience and this has brought more meaning to the work I love to do.

It is my hope and prayer that God may continue to use me to provide a place where we, the poor in spirit, can find the kingdom of heaven that is within us.

Sheila Wood

Sheila Wood lives in Manchester, England and has had a varied work career as outlined in her contribution below. She has assisted Christian Meditation coordinator John Cotling in setting up a meditation centre in Manchester and is active in sharing the "good news" of meditation in northwest England.

To tell you my story of coming to the practice of Christian Meditation I must relate a little of my early life. I am now 61 years old. I spent my childhood (in the 1940s) in a place called Hulme, in Manchester. I lived with my father and my stepmother, and my education was very basic. I was interested in all kinds of sports, especially swimming, but in my childhood I was subject to much abuse. It was a very traumatic time for me, and I now realize how it affected my later years. I grew up to be a wounded person, lacking confidence in myself and believing everyone was against me.

Life's Early Traumas

When I was 15 years old I ran away from home and lived in a hostel. Later I went to work in a clothing factory as a machinist. I then became involved with an older man, and we had a son. I later married this man, which unfortunately led me into yet another traumatic period. However, I stayed in this situation until my son was 16 years old. I then left and eventually was able to get a divorce.

The Gift of Friendship

It was during this time that changes started to happen in my life. I continued to work despite all the changes, and one day I began to talk to a man who worked in the same factory as I did. He was a kind and gentle man who was very concerned about me. To meet someone who showed real concern was a completely new experience for me. I did not understand anyone who would show kindness and expect nothing in return. I was in a really bad mental state, yet this friend was there for me.

He helped me to get on my feet again. Most important of all, he *talked* to me and *listened* to me without judging. He helped me to understand why I was so negative with myself and with others. He lent me books to read, books I had never heard of: Thomas Merton, Carlo Carretto, and Anthony de Mello, to name a few. He sometimes took me to Mass. It was because of all these experiences, and the unconditional love of my friend, that I eventually took instruction and became a member of the Catholic Church. This was the most positive and wonderful experience of my life.

Finding the True Self

In 1976 my friend sent away for the first three *Essential Teaching* cassettes on Christian Meditation by Fr. John Main and lent these tapes to me. I listened to the talks with my full attention. Although I did not fully understand what Fr. John was saying, I sensed that his teaching on meditation would allow me to find my true self. I had only known the battered self that had been locked up inside me, with all the hurt I had experienced for such a long time.

And so for the past 20 years I have listened to Fr. John's talks. I have tried to be faithful to my daily meditation. It has been a time of great revelation for me. I began slowly to have more confidence in myself, and to believe in myself. I began to feel a new freedom. I knew I had a lot of love to give, and I was beginning to want to share this love with others. I was not the worthless person that I had been led to believe I was.

"My Life Has Been Transformed through Meditation"

I eventually left my work as a machinist in the factory where I had spent 16 years and began working for the Manchester City Council Social Service. This work presented me with the privilege of caring for the sick and comforting the dying, which is the greatest gift of all. We are never closer to Jesus than when we comfort our brothers and sisters who are making their final journey.

I know now from my life experiences and from my inner experiences that it is only in giving of oneself to others, and seeking nothing in return, that we receive this overflowing abundance of love from Christ. It is his love, his energy, that he gives us to do his work. His work is love made visible and I now try to see him in everyone I meet.

My life has been transformed because of meditation. It is as though meditation, through the teaching of silence, has given me a truer understanding of myself. My self-image is no longer the serious passport pose. It is now more of a holiday snap, happy and aware that I am a tourist on a pilgrimage.

On this journey I have met so many beautiful people who have encouraged me. But I feel that it is only in sitting down to meditate, and in the experience of the practice, that we become more rooted in our true self. And it is because of this that I can give thanks and witness to Fr. John's wonderful teaching of Christian Meditation.

Serena Woon

Serena Woon lives in Palau Penang, Malaysia, where she is actively involved in sharing John Main's teaching in that country. She attended the first School for Christian Meditation Teachers held in Florence, Italy, and was recently a visiting volunteer at the Christian Meditation Centre in London, England. She has a great interest in Franciscan spirituality and has taken a six-week retreat and course on the Franciscan charism in the

Philippines. She is Malaysian Chinese but with a Taoist background and is a teacher by profession as well as a lay volunteer in a hospice home care program in Penang.

★

> *One man there had an illness which had lasted thirty-eight years, and when Jesus saw him lying there and knew he had been in that condition for a long time, he said, "Do you want to be well again?" "Sir," replied the sick man, "I have no one to put me into the pool when the water is disturbed; and while I am still on the way, someone else gets down there before me." Jesus said, "Get up, pick up your sleeping-mat and walk around." The man was cured at once, and he picked up his mat and started to walk around.*

(John 5:5-9)

I have often wondered why Jesus asked the man to pick up his sleeping-mat. Why didn't he say, "Get up and walk" as he has told others? Why is the mat so important?

"No One to Love Me"

It is only recently, when I looked at my own life, that I have been able to understand the significance of the mat. I can relate well to this sick man by the pool of Bethzatha who suffered a long time from what I would term the "no one" syndrome. His plea was "I've no one to put me into the pool," while mine was "I've no one to love me."

My concept of "no one to love me" began at an early age, when I discovered that my parents did not want me because I was a girl. All through my childhood days I not only had the feeling of being unwanted, but I developed very low self-esteem because I was brought up by a very strict and domineering mother who did not believe in dressing up a daughter. She dressed me as a boy and I was teased and laughed at by friends at school and in the neighbourhood. I was very much controlled and I had no friends to talk to.

In spite of the strict surveillance that my mother had over me, I got to know a "nice" guy and eventually got married. Sad to say, the marriage lasted only about 10 years. The man who I thought loved me turned out to be a nicer guy to another woman.

After this the "no one loves me" syndrome became so complex, like a wedge driven deep into my psyche, that my poor body could not cope any longer. About a year after my divorce I became very ill with Systemic Lupus Erythematosus (SLE). As this illness has no known cause and no medication, I was given steroids to suppress the symptoms in an effort to allow me to live a normal life.

A Taoist Healing

Seeing how ill I was, a colleague invited me one day to a church to pray for healing. I was at that time a Taoist, though I did not know a thing about Taoism. My only pious act was the burning of joss sticks on the first and fifteenth day of each lunar month. Christianity, though, was not new to me, for I was educated in a convent. Gradually I began to go to the eucharistic celebration more and more often and in 1983 I was baptized.

Christianity provided me with solace from my disappointments in life, just as my marriage had given me a reprieve from the domineering hands of my mother. Through the sacraments I experienced healing and forgiveness. Like the sick man at the pool of Bethsaida I did get up and walk.

A Thorn Piercing My Side

However, I was not walking around with freedom and ease. Like the sick man, I had to learn to walk with my mat, upon which I had been sleeping for such a long time. I know now that my mat was my "no one loves me" syndrome, which was like a thorn piercing my side all the time. Though my life had changed tremendously and I now had many friends both in and out of church, I still did not find inner peace. There was always a sense of something missing, something tugging at the inner recesses of my heart.

"Listen to the Waves, Listen to Your Heart"

I began to go for retreats to discern God's will for me and what I was to do. One day while I was praying very earnestly, I thought I heard this message: "Listen to the waves." I was in a chapel by the sea, and my first impression was that God's voice would come from the waves. How naive I was! Of course I heard nothing. As I pondered further and wondered why I heard nothing, another mysterious sentence sounded in my mind: "Listen with your heart, not with your ears." I could not make any sense of these words; neither could my spiritual director. So these words were kept in my mind and heart; I pondered them but they remained meaningless for a long time.

My experience of this inner unrest prompted my spiritual director to urge me to enter a contemplative religious order. I was very unsure whether I should, because I had already joined the secular Franciscan order. I procrastinated and then, in November 1993, something happened.

Fr. Laurence Freeman came to Malaysia and gave a two-day workshop on Christian Meditation. I listened and heard all that he said. By the time the first period of meditation was over, I was convinced that this kind of prayer was "right" for me. I can find no other words to describe why I was so steadfast in my belief.

Learning to Walk with My "Mat"

As I continue to meditate, I find that this way of prayer leads me to a "homecoming" experience. My inner restlessness has begun to abate, but what is most astonishing is that I have learned to walk about with my "mat." It is still a nuisance, but it is a happy nuisance. I have learned to look at my "no one loves me" syndrome as part of me, as something that distinguishes me from others.

Through meditation I can live in harmony with my sister donkey (that is, my body), because I have found rest in my inner being. Finding that inner harmony, which is God's gift, has helped me to look at all external things as trivial. I have found the "pearl of great price" so I can afford to sell everything to buy it, as it has transformed me from "no one" into "someone."

I am also very grateful to a dear friend who pointed out to me that "Listen to the waves" and "Listen to the sound of the mantra" are very similar. For me, now, the mystery of that message is solved. It is clear that the will of God for me is not about what I do, but who I am. There is no better way to follow God's will than to stay faithful to the two periods of meditation as I sit in stillness and in silence listening to the sound of the mantra.

Chapter 8

The Fruits of Meditation

"A Change Has Taken Place in Me"

Peter Collins
Karen Deley
Hilda Frost
Irene Koroi
Bob Lukey
Mary Lou McCluskey
Evelyn McDevitt
Carol Peterson

Peter Collins

Peter Collins was born in Moodiesburn, Scotland, in 1962 and lives with his wife and five daughters near Kemptville, Ontario, Canada. He works as an exploration geologist and is editor of the Benedictine oblate newsletter Via Vitae.

Years ago I attended charismatic prayer meetings at our parish centre. At one such meeting a friend of mine, inspired by the Spirit, began to speak a prophetic word. The message was simple and to the point: "I, Jesus, desire from you a still greater commitment, that our friendship may grow." Although uttered in a group setting, the words, strangely enough, touched me at a very personal level. For some time I questioned how I could further commit myself to Jesus, given my state of life with a young family and a demanding job.

In addition, I had begun to pray regularly, read spiritual books and attend prayer meetings and Mass as often as I could. What did Jesus want of me? To run off and join a monastery? I resisted confiding to my wife about the matter as she didn't quite share my new-found enthusiasm for the spiritual life. Indeed, as I look back I can certainly see how my zealous behaviour got on her nerves a bit, especially regarding the charismatic involvement. "It's just not for you," she would often tell me. Quite frankly, she was right.

"A Way out of the Inner Darkness"

I'm convinced that the charismatic experience deepened my faith in God and helped me to pray better. However, I didn't feel truly at home there. In fact, the moments I preferred the most at the meetings were the brief yet profoundly silent ones when all the singing and chatter would cease. Furthermore, I was increasingly attracted to the contemplative life in the church, mainly through the writings of Thomas Merton.

Nevertheless, the same week that I heard the aforementioned message, our parish priest, Fr. Lynett, visited our home. He brought a set of tapes entitled *Silence, Stillness, and Simplicity* by Fr. Laurence

Freeman for me to listen to. Walt was very excited by the message of the tapes. He had been going through a real crisis in his own prayer life, which he once described as "desperate," and Christian Meditation seemed to be a way out of that inner darkness. He spoke to me as though he had found a pearl of great price that he wanted to share with me. That evening I listened with joy to the tapes and without hesitation began the routine of meditating mornings and evenings. The clincher was hearing Laurence on the tapes say that meditation leads one to a great commitment to Jesus.

The Certainty of Love

That moment of knowing or revelation reminded me of how I felt on my first date with my wife, Brenda. As teenagers we went skating on the Rideau Canal in Ottawa during a winter carnival. Within the first few hours of being together we each knew intuitively that we would one day commit ourselves to marriage. We had fallen in love. In a similar way, I embarked on the journey of meditation with a certainty that this was a way of prayer in which I felt very much at home.

The Fruits of Meditation

The experience of meditation has taught me how to seek true love in all aspects of my life and in the lives of others. Meditation is the gentle hand that gathers the scattered pieces of a puzzling life and creates a coherent picture of who I am. It also initiates clearer insights as to who I AM is. The mantra is like a neutralizing agent that distils the dualistic nature and narrow-minded prejudices of the ego. No longer do I find my way of thinking to be strictly divided along lines of right vs wrong or secular vs spiritual and so on.

Through meditation, the Spirit has taught me to be more tolerant and respectful of another point of view if it differs markedly from mine and to be aware of my own goodness and capacity for love. In addition, I feel I have a keener sense of my many failings of character and spirit and how they affect those around me. Yet I am more accepting and patient with myself than I used to be. I can usually predict when my stubborn ego is about to rear its ugly head and I try to subdue it beforehand. However, if the Spirit can't get through to me, then Brenda certainly will!

Meditation and Becoming a Better Parent

Meditation, I think, has helped me to be a better parent. Since I now have a better understanding of the workings of my psyche, I feel I can discern and sympathize with the various stages of life as my children experience them. Often when we pray together as a family, many of the hurts and joys of the day are discussed and resolved. Praying together facilitates the desire to share thoughts and feelings we would otherwise repress and helps to keep the lines of communication open, which is vital for happy family living. Lately we try to include a few minutes of silent meditation with each family prayer session. As my two eldest daughters encounter the difficult adolescent years I feel the need to meditate is stronger than ever as I enter a new phase of parenthood. Lord, help me!

"Circumstances Beyond Our Control"

The fruits of meditation help us to make sense of and derive good from the dark times we experience in life. For example, when we are in conflict with another, or faced with the illness or death of a loved one, unemployment or our own failing health, the practice of meditation teaches us to be more patient and accepting of circumstances beyond our control. I was diagnosed with multiple sclerosis several years ago, and to my surprise I remained calm and thereafter sought natural ways to help my body defend against MS attacks. My good friend and fellow meditator Fr. Lynett recently received news that he has throat cancer; he also believes that meditation has helped him remain composed and confident in this time of personal crisis.

The City of God Within

In a nutshell, meditation allows us to be more fully aware of the presence of God in our life. In a special way we can touch the humanity of Jesus and acquire an appreciation of his family life at Nazareth where he lived with his mother, father, friends, neighbours, and so on. Holiness is therefore the vocation of all people and not just a chosen few. The school of holiness is *life* itself, the teacher abides in our hearts and love is learned and experienced in the ordinary circumstances of everyday living. Meditation is a tool of the monastery which the lay person can take home and use to build a contemplative community without walls, yet with a universal foundation. The discipline of the practice undermines the old architecture designed by the false self and erects in its place a dwelling for the true self, a city of God within. John Main has presented us with the key to that city. The rest is up to us.

Karen Deley

Karen Deley lives in Winnipeg, Manitoba, Canada, and is married with three children. She is an Anglican, a coordinator for Christian Meditation in Manitoba and an oblate of St. Benedict's monastery in Winnipeg, where she recently completed the first phase of a spiritual formation program.

I was first introduced to Christian Meditation about 13 years ago. A friend told me that a Benedictine monk, Laurence Freeman, was coming to St. Benedict's monastery in Winnipeg to give a talk and so I attended.

Before going to this talk I had begun meditating using the word "Jesus" as my mantra. For the first six months I found this way of prayer extremely difficult. Quieting the body of twitches and the mind of distracting images and anxieties was a great challenge. However, when I heard Fr. Laurence speak about John Main's teaching and the Christian tradition of meditation, I had an overwhelming experience that I had arrived *home* and that this was a spiritual path for the rest of my life, although not an easy path.

After a few years of attending a group at St. Benedict's, I was asked to give a talk on Christian Meditation at my own church.

With much trepidation I agreed; this eventually led to starting a group in my own Anglican parish.

"If No One Else Came I Would Give Up"

Within the year only two people remained in this group and I became discouraged. One night I came to the conclusion that if no one else came to the group I would give up. On that particular evening my husband, Michael, came with me and that same night our parish minister decided to attend. Before long the number of members grew rapidly and I was approached by another church to start a group. There are now 40 members in that group.

I led both groups for six months and then I was inundated by requests to give talks and write articles on Christian Meditation for a variety of newspapers and newsletters. With the support of our Anglican bishop, Patrick Lee, I have begun to give a series of courses on meditation for the Anglican diocese of Ruperts Land. I'm also editor for a Manitoba Christian Meditation newsletter, which goes out twice a year to members of the 18 meditation groups in this part of Canada. We are fortunate to have a variety of speakers visit Winnipeg, including Fr. Laurence Freeman and Paul Harris.

Learning to Live in the Present Moment

The practice of Christian Meditation has transformed my life. In the beginning I was timid, fearful, full of anxiety and doubtful about using my talents to share the teaching. Through the discipline of the daily practice I have learned to live in the present moment, to trust in the *inner Christ*, and to share the gift with others without fear. I am sensitive to the presence of Jesus in my daily life and to the guidance of the Holy Spirit.

My, How You've Changed

After meditating for only a few years, I one day went to my family doctor for a medical check-up. He said to me, "What has happened to you? You're a different person. You've changed." He wasn't referring to any physical change but to the change in my *inner* being. He noticed, as I have, my inner change to a person who is more alive and full of faith.

I feel the key to John Main's teaching is his insistence on returning to the mantra no matter how many times our mind wanders or we are distracted. His books and tapes are also important in *keeping* us on the path.

The role of the weekly meditation group in nurturing meditation and introducing new people to meditation is another key to the spread of the teaching. The weekly meeting gives us support from fellow travellers on the same journey. We meet others who are struggling, and in sharing the difficulties and the challenge of keeping on the path, we gain new strength and encouragement to carry on.

Hilda Frost

Sr. Hilda Frost is a Benedictine sister of St. Benedict's Monastery, Winnipeg, Canada. She originally came from St. Scholastica's Abbey, Teignmouth, England. Hilda has been practising Christian Meditation for about 25 years, is now one of the coordinators for Christian Meditation in Winnipeg and gives retreats and workshops on this way of contemplative prayer.

I don't think there was ever a time in my life when I was not interested in contemplative prayer and meditation, even though it was only later that I came into contact with John Main's writings. At a very early age I learned from my Congregationalist mother and my Methodist father how to pray and to love the scriptures. When I was a child we mostly attended the Anglican church, which has always been dear to me. I went to school at a Catholic convent, and at the age of 16 decided to become a Catholic. I then entered the Benedictines in England shortly after I turned 21.

As a Benedictine novice and community member I was fortunate in having many opportunities to pursue scripture and monastic studies, which have stood me in good stead ever since. Over the years the teaching of Benedict, together with that of the mystics across the centuries, has become very important to me. I became a fan of Thomas Merton, and later also of John Main, when I discovered his writings. The thing that appealed to me about John Main's teaching was its rootedness in and connectedness to the scriptures and to centuries of contemplative prayer in the church.

"Being" Rather than "Doing"

I was also impressed by the utter simplicity of John Main's approach: repeating a mantra or prayer word throughout the time of meditation, morning and evening. There were no complicated formulas to follow, no unreal expectations set down, no yardstick or criteria to establish whether I had got it right. For me, <u>meditation has always been a matter of *being* rather than *doing*</u>: a loving attentiveness in the presence of God who, even in the midst of distractions, "enfolds us in love," as Julian of Norwich would say. Along with meditation there is also the close association with *Lectio Divina* or holy reading of scripture, which also speaks meaningfully to me and nourishes me spiritually.

From England to Canada

After living more than 20 years as a Benedictine in England, I found myself in a small and diminished community, which eventually closed due to lack of members. In 1981 I transferred to St. Benedict's here in Canada. Much to my delight, about 15 years ago Fr. Laurence Freeman was invited to preach our community retreat. This gave me a first-hand opportunity to learn even more about meditation, to deepen my personal commitment to it, and to become more involved in spreading the good news here in Winnipeg and beyond through retreats and talks.

Meditation has become such an essential part of my life that I could not live without it. Despite my own limitations, failings and vulnerability, I have experienced the fruits of meditation in my own life, especially that of a joyful and even fun-loving spirit, which is surely the mark of the followers of Christ. If we are going to be prophets at all, let us be joyful ones, not prophets of gloom!

Friendship and Bonding Through Meditation

One of the many blessings that involvement in meditation brings is that of friendship. I have found a truly loving, warm acceptance among those who gather, either regularly in a meditation group or for retreats and workshops. I experience a real bonding with all of them, especially in an ecumenical sense. The World Community for Christian Meditation unites us all, and is a much-valued means of communication and support.

For me, meditation is not only a link with Christians of all denominations, but goes far beyond that to those of other world religions. Through the writings of Bede Griffiths (a Benedictine monk who spent more than 30 years in India) in particular, I have come to appreciate that as meditators we can also share with followers of non-Christian religions, and that we can enrich each other.

"Becoming One with the One Who Is One"

As Fr. Laurence says, "Through meditation we become one with the One Who is One." I believe that contemplative prayer is God's gift to the church and to the world. Through the inspiration of John Main's teaching, contemplative prayer has been brought within the reach of everyone: lay people, sisters and priests alike. It is no longer restricted to monks, nuns or a few "holy" people, but has become an essential part of the lives of countless people all over the world. Gradually, the Spirit is leading us to that contemplative renewal that John Main dreamed of during his lifetime, and which since his death is spreading among all people and all nations.

Irene Koroi

Irene Koroi is a widow with seven children ranging in age from 10 to 32 years, and lives in Suva, the capital of Fiji. Her husband died in a car crash when her youngest daughter was 10 months old. She has 11 grandchildren with another one on the way. Irene leads a Christian Meditation group of indigenous Fijians in Suva.

My personal journey to the practice of Christian Meditation probably started in early childhood. It is really amazing that what one encounters in childhood is often the basis of where one will be eventually led in adulthood. From my childhood I have fond memories of my parents. My mother was a very ill and very brave woman. She contracted leprosy and had to be isolated to a leper island in the Fiji Islands group. Meanwhile, they sent my sister and me to a boarding school. I was six and my sister was four. Our family was reunited when they healed mum of the disease four years later.

My parents were devout Catholics. Mum had a Fijian translation of a book on spirituality. It must have been a book concerning *lectio divina*. She was very attached to this book, which was big and looked like a Bible. She sewed a green cover for it. I used to observe her, despite the pain, being faithful to her daily prayer life commitment. Dad was the same. We lived in a humble tin shack but my mother made it into a shrine. On Christmas Eve, we couldn't go to midnight mass because of mum's infirmities, but she nevertheless would lovingly prepare an altar. Then she would bring out of her trunk the nativity scene which she kept between layers of clothing. They would wake us up at midnight and then we would all say our prayers together and sing Christmas carols. The disease badly deformed mum's hands and legs. Mum died of cancer at the age of 43. She left us her legacy, though. The Fijian word for meditation is *Meditasio*. Mum planted the seed of meditation in my heart when I was 10 years old. It took 40 years to germinate. This was the *word* that made a lasting impression in my mind.

Involvement in Charismatic Renewal

In 1980 my eldest daughter was a senior at a Catholic secondary school in Suva, which is the capital city of Fiji. The Sisters of St. Joseph De Cluny run this school. The principal of the school had asked the students to invite their parents to the Catholic charismatic convention, which they held at the school during the weekend. She came home and told us about it. In fact, this was the first time that we had heard the word "charismatic." This word became part of our lives for the next decade. We became actively involved in the Catholic charismatic renewal in the archdiocese, convening and giving Life in the Spirit seminars. After the death of my husband, I took on the leadership in our parish. I became an editor/presenter of the charismatic newsletter *The Harvest*.

It was through the Catholic charismatic renewal that the seed of meditation already planted in my heart sprouted to life. In 1992, three of us from our parish prayer group attended a Catholic charismatic convention in Brisbane, Australia. On the lists of workshops that they conducted was one on Christian Meditation. Fr. Laurence Freeman was giving the workshop. As I recall, this was the workshop that had the most participants. Afterwards there was a long queue of people who wanted to see him. I managed to have a short conversation with Fr. Laurence. I told him that I believed the Lord took me from my own little island in Fiji to Australia to attend his workshop on Christian Meditation. Fr. Laurence asked us to put down our names so we could get the International Christian Meditation Newsletter.

Friends Joined the Group

When I returned home I began to meditate as Fr. Laurence had taught us: 30 minutes in the morning and 30 minutes in the evening, *Maranatha*. I was very enthusiastic. I started to share Christian Meditation with some of our charismatic prayer group members. By this time the newsletter from England started arriving. Three women friends started to join me for meditation. A new priest, Fr.

Denis Mahony, was now posted to the Wailekutu Prayer Centre. The Marist Fathers are in charge of this centre. It is just a 15-minute drive from the city. I sometimes go to the centre for prayer in the chapel or just to rest.

On one of my trips to the centre, I made an appointment with Fr. Denis. He listened attentively to everything I shared with him. He was very excited about it. He told me that for the past few years he had been trying to start a contemplative prayer group. My speaking with him was a sign to him that the time was right for Christian Meditation to be introduced to our people. This was in 1994. He ran a course for about 15 of us for 13 weeks, after which he formed three groups. Now, three years later, 12 groups meet every week.

Coming Home after a Long Journey

For me, Christian Meditation is like "coming home after a long journey." I have found the pearl of great price. Meditation is like breathing and eating for me. Two months ago I bought myself a timer, so I must be very serious about my commitment to meditation now! Sometimes, because of the noise from the traffic, it is very difficult for me to meditate. Nevertheless, it seems that I have learned to accept this noise as part of my meditation practice and commitment.

Our group meets at the sacristy of the Sacred Heart Cathedral every Thursday afternoon. Seven of us are committed and attend every week. Ever since we started three years ago, about 60 people from the greater Suva area have come to meditate with us. Some have gone on to other groups and two have started their own group. Fr. Denis Mahony is a great help to all of us. He supplies us with tapes and books and is our spiritual director and a friend to all our meditation families in Fiji. There is a box of tissues in his small living room, where we share our life, aspirations and hurts; the box of tissues comes in very handy. I have found that meditation heals at every level of our life. Christian Meditation is a gift from God to those who are seekers. Jesus says, *"Seek and you shall find, knock and the door shall be opened to you."* (Matthew 7:7)

Bob Lukey

Bob Lukey, who lives in Flemington, a suburb of Melbourne, Australia, is married and now retired. He spends his spare time as loan librarian for the Australian Christian Meditation network and as a palliative care volunteer in Melbourne.

Some years ago a man came to our little Anglican church on a Sunday night to take part in the evening service. Although he was not of our tradition, he came to visit us because very few churches are open on Sunday evenings. He became aware of my love of silence and one week brought a set of three tapes by Fr. John Main entitled *The Essential Teaching* and lent them to me. Immediately upon listening to Fr. John's talks I knew that this was to be my spiritual path. From that day on, the twice-daily discipline of meditation recommended by Fr. John has been an essential part of my spiritual pilgrimage.

After a number of years as a member of the Australian meditation community, I decided to offer to take over the care and distribution of our Christian Meditation library of tapes and books. At that time some 50 meditators used our loan service. We now have over 200 meditators across Australia using our library; six to 12 packets of tapes or other material arrive in the mail on most days of the week. How blessed it is to meet and in many cases to correspond with these meditators all over this huge country. Often I start work in the office very early in the morning to handle the workload. Rather than finding the work in any way onerous, I must say that having responsibility of lending our books and tapes is a labour of great joy.

Quite Old but Wise

Quite a few dear people who use the library live in very isolated places, and their letters often reflect a great loneliness. Indeed, in many instances people will write about a personal problem that has no connection with meditation, and they are pleased to share their difficulty with someone they are never likely to meet in the flesh. Many of our long-time borrowers have come to know that the librarian is quite old but may be wise enough to answer their questions.

Fr. John Main reminds us many times that we are not to expect anything to "happen" in our meditation, but in faith and trust we are to say our word for the two periods of our meditation every day. As we go along the path we may well be directed by the Holy Spirit into unexpected activities. An apparently chance meeting with another person may indicate to us a certain avenue we must explore.

Some years ago a young lady came to our church. She was a district nurse and in conversation mentioned that her organization had set up a palliative care service for terminally ill patients (by the way, she borrowed our John Main tapes for her own use). She was looking for volunteers mainly in a "respite" capacity, to give the caregiver, usually a wife or mother, a break for a couple of hours once each week, and to enable the caregiver to get away from the 24-hour-a-day responsibility. This volunteer work seemed to fit perfectly with my daily discipline of meditation and seems a natural overflow of the fruits of meditation. St. Paul mentioned love as the first fruit of prayer: love for oneself, God and others.

Distractions: Just Ignore Them

In many of the letters that come to me from meditators in Australia, I have the opportunity to assist with difficulties that these people meet from time to time as they travel along the path. It may be useful for me to share one or two of these solutions. Meditators often mention that when they have been on this sometimes rocky road of meditation for a while, occasionally one distraction will stick out above the others. It may well be a persistent sound that seems to override their saying and listening to the word. Certainly there is no quick or easy answer to this; once again, the key is perseverance. Some would say that it will take a lifetime to attain a settled and still heart. As one continues along the daily path of meditation, this dominant distraction will fade or shrivel up. As an English meditator says in the wonderful video *Coming Home*, "Distractions? Just ignore them."

In one of his books, Fr. John puts it beautifully when he compares the journey of meditation to water in a glass; for as the particles settle the water becomes clearer and clearer, and becomes sparkling clear water that allows light to pass through without any obstruction. Fr. John's favourite advice, so often noted on his tapes and in his books, is this saying: "In your own experience." In meditation we do come to experience the darkness and the difficulties as well as the sunshine and joy.

However, a common question still asked by meditators and dealt with so well by Fr. John and other teachers of the discipline is this: "How long is it going to take me?" The fact is we never *arrive*. We just say our word, and the experience of the discipline of meditation provides the answer to this question. More and more wonder, peace and joy in our lives *will* gradually be revealed to us as we say our word morning and night with fidelity. This has been my great experience.

Mary Lou McCluskey

Mary Lou McCluskey lives in Sydney, Nova Scotia, Canada, is married to Terry and has four children. She has a B.Sc. in biology and is working towards a B.A. degree in theology and philosophy. Mary Lou is the Christian Meditation coordinator for Cape Breton, Nova Scotia.

When I initially was invited to contribute to this book, I wanted to find some dark corner and hide. On second thought, I decided to try to write my story to encourage others. I am the "unfaithful" faithful one. Some weeks I meditate twice a week, others as frequently as five times, rarely twice a day, and when life gets hectic

I might even stop for a while. But I always come back to meditating. I need it as much as I need air to breathe. Even in my unfaithfulness, meditation is a very important part of me. It is because I believe that others also struggle with unfaithfulness that I am writing this reflection.

I started to meditate in the late 1970s. I had read a few books by Thomas Merton on contemplation, and I had also read *The Way of a Pilgrim*. In this latter book, the Jesus Prayer was used. Then I read *The Cloud of Unknowing*. As a result of my reading, I tried to meditate using the Jesus Prayer as my mantra. This process went on sporadically for a little over 10 years. I received no encouragement from priests. Instead I was told that it would be better to pray matins and lauds each day. Since both prayer forms are time-consuming, they began to compete with each other.

Four years ago we had a change in pastors. Fr. Norman McPhee came to our parish. He had been practising meditation for several years as set out by Fr. John Main. He invited the parishioners to attend an introductory prayer meeting. The rest, as they say, is history.

Well, not quite. The following fall I went to a St. Vincent de Paul conference in Halifax, where Paul Harris spoke on John Main and Christian Meditation. A few months later, at my invitation, he gave the annual St. Vincent de Paul's retreat day to the Vincentians and to other people from Cape Breton interested in meditation.

Getting My Prayer Act Together

I think I need to explain why I have such a difficult time getting my prayer act together. First, I am not a morning person. Second, I take medicine which makes it difficult to wake up in the morning. To rise before 8:30 AM is a gift from God. Once I'm up, I take over an hour to get into motion. I am studying for my B.A. in theology and philosophy. Two mornings a week I have classes, and then I spend all afternoon and all day Saturday working on my courses. I try not to study on Sunday or during the evenings; these are set aside for relaxation and to attend meetings. I stop studying at 5:00 PM and I am frequently out the door by 7:00 PM. I do not meditate after nine in the evening as it wakes me up, and I need to be in bed by 10:30 PM. Yet somewhere in that schedule I do manage to meditate, albeit irregularly.

"Wasting Time" with God

As irregular as I am in meditating daily, I know this prayer form is essential to me. I believe in prayer. I believe that it is the most important thing I do. Prayer leads to fruitful action. St. Paul counsels us to pray always, and meditation may be considered a form of continuous prayer. We sit in our place of prayer and spend the time "wasting time with God," as my pastor likes to put it. I start the meditation period saying the Our Father in rhythm with my breathing. Then I turn to the mantra, *Maranatha*. I pray the word slowly and try to allow for a little space at the end of each breath. Sometimes I have a little silence and then the distractions occur. Through all the noise I try not to lose my word. Frankly, I do not really worry if my mind is cluttered or not. Silence, or stillness, is God's gift to us, not our accomplishment. The important thing is that I take time for God.

I have a very noisy mind. This is partly due to the the fact that I am a manic-depressive. I have had this illness for over 25 years and it strongly influences my thought patterns. When I am in a manic phase, the ideas pour into my mind like a flood, not only in number but also in force. When I am depressed, the ideas are negative and non-redemptive. However, most of my life is quite normal, full of a steady flow of ideas that should be thought about at some time, but not during meditation. At all times I must work hard to concentrate on my word. Ma-ra-na-tha. Over and over. And God comes.

A Change Has Taken Place in Me

Oh, I cannot say that I hear him, feel him or see him, but I know that he comes. My life has become different. I have been on medication for years, but these last three years are different. I am definitely more patient. I am capable in a way that I was not before. In fact I have a little success story to share with you. Five years ago, in the spring, the Catholic Women's League asked if I would chair their social justice committee. I was thrilled and agreed to do so. When the fall came I was too overwhelmed to do the job and, much to my chagrin, passed in my resignation. A little over three years ago I became president of the St. Vincent de Paul Society. I have just completed my term. It is the first time in my life that I have ever held office. I think that I have done a fair job at it as well. The inner confidence that I needed to do this job was and is, for me, a gift from God. A change has taken place in me.

Fr. John Main and Fr. Laurence Freeman tell us not to expect anything to happen while we are meditating. Now, if they are referring to visions or voices or the like, they are quite right. However, we must expect *something*. What is the purpose of prayer if you do not expect to interact with God at your deepest level? Meditation permits God to move from that level into all the empty spaces of your being.

It Doesn't Happen Overnight

I really believe that through meditation we are united to God in a unique way. We open ourselves to God and his divine will for us. As a result, in our everyday life we start making different, more positive decisions than before. We act differently; we truly become Christians. Unfortunately, all this does not happen overnight, and we are not the first to see it happening in us. It is our family and friends who first see the changes that are occurring because of our new prayer life. I know that this has happened to me.

The other most wonderful experience I have had through this prayer is the experience of being *loved by God*. Because I know how much God loves me, I know how much he loves and cherishes the world. I am humbled before him.

I thank God for meditation and hope that God will give me the grace to persevere on the journey forward.

Evelyn McDevitt

Sr. Evelyn McDevitt is a Sister of Mercy in Belfast, Northern Ireland. She was born in Sligo, went to school with the St. Louis sisters in Monoghan, and at 18 years of age trained as a nurse at Mater Hospital, Belfast. She is now Christian Meditation coordinator and spends much of her time organizing seminars, retreats, starting new groups and strengthening the 24 existing meditation groups in Northern Ireland.

With the joy of having received a great gift, I would like to share a little of my spiritual journey, up to the time I came in contact with the practice of Christian Meditation. The seeds of spirituality in my life were sown by my parents and nourished by school, church and real-life experience. I was exposed early in my life to a simple, unsophisticated brand of Irish spirituality with daily Mass, family rosary and weekly confession. My faith was strong and, from an early age, I was aware of an *invisible* God. I continued, though, to search, thirst and long for a deeper understanding and experience of Christ.

I read all the books I could get my hands on, such as St. John of the Cross, Teresa of Avila and Thomas Merton, in an attempt to find this inner Christ. I loved scripture and read and reflected on it faithfully every day. The essential scriptures that were in my heart at this time were *"My whole being yearns and pines for Yahweh's courts, my heart and my body cry out for you to the living God"* (Psalm 84:1-2) and *"O God, hear my cry, listen to my prayer; from the end of the earth I call to you with fainting heart."* (Psalm 61:1-2)

A Kind of Spiritual Death

Nevertheless, despite my spiritual yearnings, I felt at times God's apparent absence from my life. It seemed to me I was always drifting further and further away from him. Life at this time was dull and flat, including spiritual exhaustion and burnout. Everything seemed empty to me, and it was a kind of spiritual death. In spite of how I felt, I always kept up a good front, but deep inside I was in agony. This also made me feel false, not real. Like most people I went through a dark period. Some call it the desert experience; St. John of the Cross speaks about the dark night of the soul. I felt this was the great death prior to awakening.

After many years, I was on a directed retreat when scripture suddenly came alive to me. The text that touched me very deeply was *"That they may have life and have it to the full!"* (John 10:10). *A veil was torn away from my eyes in a flash, and all I can say is "I was blind, now I see"* (John 9:25); *"[That he called me] out of darkness into his marvellous light"* (1 Peter 2:9); and *"I was lost and was found."* (Luke 15:32)

In this retreat it was as if I had been asleep all my life and had just awakened. There was a sense of living in a new world. Nature also came alive for me and was a source of great comfort. Scripture became more vibrant and meaningful. I just fell at God's feet in wonder and joy bubbled within me.

The Mantra Is Where the Great Secret Lies

Having retired from nursing and pastoral care, I felt the call to a deeper prayer life. I was looking for something I could share with others. I asked my superior if I could take a three-month sabbatical to discover for myself what form this should take. I went to Hawkstone Hall Pastoral Centre in Shrewsbury, England, run by the Redemptorist fathers. It was here that I was introduced to Christian Meditation.

That does not mean that I had not already heard of Fr. John Main or Fr. Laurence Freeman. I had actually read some of their books and had tried several times to pray using a mantra without success. My problem was, I discovered later, that I did not really know the proper teaching of the mantra. To me this is where the great secret lies.

It is the saying of the mantra over and over for the whole period of the meditation (20 to 30 minutes) and listening to the sound of it that brings you into the silence. I did a meditation workshop for three months, which was led by meditator and teacher Leslie Glaze.

At first I experienced great difficulty in letting go of thoughts and images, even thoughts of God. In the beginning I felt I was pushing God away by using the mantra. I had loved reflecting on scripture and being present to God in nature, so it was hard for me to let go of images, words and thoughts. I explained this to Leslie. He very gently encouraged me to try a little longer and be patient. I can honestly say that was the best direction I have ever received.

Stillness Is the Womb of Great Achievements

I kept at the meditation morning and evening, and after a few months I experienced a great power and strength in myself. The doctrine of the indwelling Christ came alive for me. I also experienced a new-found compassion, great tenderness and sensitivity. I felt I was given a share in his divine love, and this gave me immeasurable peace. To quote St. Thomas Aquinas, "All was like straw that went before." Silence purified and removed all the obstacles that were preventing me from loving God, others and myself. An English Dominican, Gerald Vann, wrote, "Stillness is the womb of great achievements." You just cannot understand the sheer magnificence and wonder of it. As scripture says, *"It's no longer our prayer but the spirit prays in us."* (Romans 8:26)

This does not mean that all was rosy in the spiritual garden. I still had much suffering in my life. I had surgery for cancer followed by chemotherapy, but my faith and experience of God, through prayer, were a wonderful support.

I really fell into this type of prayer because of its utter simplicity. It did require a certain amount of effort but the weekly meditation group meetings were a great support. Eventually the effort became almost effortless and the mantra became rooted in the ground of my being. Grace seemed to work in an invisible fashion. The reward of my journey is to go on travelling, the solace of searching is to go on searching, for there is no end to my journey this side of eternity.

Helping to Generate Peace

When I returned from England, following my three-month sabbatical, I immediately started a group in my own convent and have been forming groups with the help of other meditators ever since. We now have 24 groups in Northern Ireland and I am hoping that this way of prayer will, in some way, help to generate peace here.

I thank God for the transformation I have experienced in my life through Christian Meditation and for the support and encouragement I received from Fr. Laurence, Leslie Glaze, Paul Harris and many meditators here in Northern Ireland.

"Glory be to Him, whose power working in me can do infinitely more than I can ask or imagine." (Ephesians 4:26)

Carol Peterson

Carol Peterson, an Anglican, is married and lives in Thessalon in northern Ontario, Canada. She is a Christian Meditation coordinator in that area and runs a John Main tape rental service from her home. Carol has meditated since 1980 and has organized various meditation conferences in northern Ontario.

I met John Main and Laurence Freeman in 1980, when they were giving a lecture series in our suburb of Montreal. I had been practising various forms of prayer and meditation, yet something always seemed to be missing. I always felt on the fringe of the authentic. I was both surprised and overjoyed to hear of a practice of meditation in the Christian tradition, taught by Benedictine monks.

For the next 18 months, I attended the weekly meditation group at the Montreal Priory. What I found there was an accepting and loving community of people. They opened the doors to me, even when I arrived late on a rainy night, and they listened to my questions. John Main's words about rediscovering our roots and rooting the mantra in our hearts spoke to me in a very personal way. Encouragement from Bishop Henry Hill, the retired Anglican Bishop of Ontario who was living at the Priory, and the sudden death of my older brother, called me to return to my own roots in the Anglican faith.

In 1982 we moved to Ontario, and I connected with the Toronto community. I joined a weekly meditation group and met monthly with either John Main or Laurence Freeman. Fr. John's death at the end of that year was a great shock and sorrow to everyone. However, it encouraged us to carry on, to share the gift of the teaching he had given us. We met and meditated in small community groups, and at international seminars, conferences and retreats.

Moving again, this time to northern Ontario and further from a home base, I met new friends and meditators, and experienced again that same sense of belonging to a loving, caring community, working together to practise and to share the teaching.

The John Main Tape Rental Program

At one of the conferences a tape rental program was started to provide the John Main talks on meditation to the new groups spreading out across Canada. I eventually took over this program, and immediately discovered a whole new medium of communication. In mailings going out to a wide variety of people, we often exchanged notes of gratitude, encouragement and support. The communal sharing and love I had experienced in the past were taking on a new shape. When we met at a conference or retreat, it was always with great joy and surprise that we put a face to the name of one of the tape subscribers. Then came the idea of offering the Music/Silence/Music timing tapes, providing yet another opportunity to communicate and connect with others on the path.

A Monastery Without Walls

At the John Main Seminar in 1991, Fr. Bede Griffiths introduced us to the Monastery Without Walls and the formation of the World Community for Christian Meditation. I no longer belonged to a weekly meditation group, but became a "cell of one." With the tape program and the conferences and retreats, I was still very much connected to this expanding community of love.

The 1994 seminar with the Dalai Lama in London, England, was a mountaintop experience for me. The Christian Meditation community was reaching out to other faiths, discovering a depth of Spirit and binding us together in the unity of silence.

Silence Does Lead to Service

In the years since meeting Fr. John, we have all gone through inevitable changes. This is what strikes me, that we are all beginners, that we are always beginning again each day. No matter how far in distance we are from each other, we are all intimately connected in the one Spirit through the practice of meditation. We all have an important place and we all play out our role in the building up of this community of love. As a fellow pilgrim, Gerry Pierse, said in the title of one of his books, "Silence does lead to service."

Contributors grouped by countries

England

Robbie Bishop
Len Connor
John Cotling
Joyce Donaghue
Madeleine Simon
David Wood
Sheila Wood

Ireland (The Republic and Northern Ireland)

Elizabeth Byrnes
Yvonne (Main) Fitzgerald
Evelyn McDevitt
Antoinette O'Reilly
Sheila Walshe

Canada

Tom Cain
Peter Collins
Dorothy Deakin
Karen Deley
Hilda Frost
Lionel F. Goulet

Mary Lou McCluskey
Isobel Page
Carol Peterson
Henri Tardy

United States

Joseph L. Barcello
Nina Carpenter
Steve Cartwright
Frank Cassidy
Peter A. De Marco
Joe Doerfer
Ed Falchiere
Julie F. Felton
Sheila Geary
Patricia Gulick
John Jay Hughes
Nancy Kadrovach
Suzy T. Kane
Pat Kasmarik
David A. Kruse
James Logan
William Mishler
Boyne Norton
Mary Orth-Pallavicini
Gregory J. Ryan
Frank Seeburger
Marlene Sweeney
Seraphim Thomas
Donna Wojtyna

Fiji

Irene Koroi
Denise McMahon
Denis Mahony

Malaysia

Serena Woon

Malta

Frank Delia

Australia

Maurie Costello
Al of Hobart
Bob Lukey
Carol McDonough
Michael Mifsud
Leon Milroy
Jo Russell
Judi Taylor
Katharine Thomas

The World Community for Christian Meditation

Meditation is the tradition of the early Christian monks and, as John Main passed it on, has led to the formation of a worldwide community of meditators in over 90 countries. Well over 1000 groups meet each week. An International Directory is maintained at the Community's International Centre in London. A Guiding Board oversees the direction of the Community, a quarterly newsletter, the annual John Main Seminar, the School for Teachers, and the co-ordination of the Christian Meditation Centres around the world.

Christian Meditation Centres

International Centre

23 Kensington Square
London W8 5HN
U.K.
Tel: 44 171 937 4679
Fax: 44 171 937 6790
E-mail: wccm@compuserve.com

Australia

Australia Christian Meditation Community
P.O. Box 6630
St. Kilda Road
Central Victoria 3004
Tel/Fax: 61 7 3300 3873 or 61 3 9435 8943
E-mail: acmchall@Bigpond.com

Belgium

Christelijk Meditatie Centrum
Beiaardlaan 1
1850 Grimbergen
Tel: 32 2 269 5071
E-mail: dhooghedumon@planetinternet.be

Brazil

Crista Meditacao Comunidade
CP 33266
CEP 22442-970
Rio de Janiero RJ
Tel: 55 21 512 3806
Fax: 55 21 294 7995
E-mail: smorais@ibm.net

Canada

Christian Meditation Centre
P.O. Box 552, Station NDG
Montreal, Quebec H4A 3P9
Tel: 1 514 766 0475
Fax: 1 514 937 8178
E-mail: mark.schofield@sympatico.ca

Centre de Méditation Chrétienne
Cap-Vie
367 Boulevard Ste-Rose
Laval, Quebec H7I 1N3
Tel: 1 450 625 0133

Germany

Zentrum für Christliche Meditation
Postfach 122045
68071 Mannheim
Tel: 49 171 268 6245
Fax: 49 171 13 268 6245
E-mail: WCCM-D@t-online.de

India

Christian Meditation Centre
1/1429 Bilathikulam Road
Calicut
673006 Kerala
Tel: 91 33 495 50395

Ireland

Christian Meditation Centre
4 Eblana Avenue
Dun Laoghaire
Co. Dublin
Tel: 353 1 280 1505
Fax: 353 1 280 8720

Italy

Centro de Meditazione Christiana
Abbazia de San Miniato al Monte
Via Delle Porte Sante 34
50125 Firenze
Tel/Fax: 39 055 247 6302

Malaysia

Christian Meditation Community
7 Jalan Pekaka Dua
Sg. Dua Gelogor
Pulau Pinang 11700
Tel: 60 4 657 7414
E-mail: saymooi@tm.net.my

New Zealand

Christian Meditation Community
PO Box 28-084
Kelburn, Wellington
Tel: 64 4 475 7847
Fax: 64 4 475 7398
E-mail: clarkerr@xtra.co.nz

Philippines

Christian Meditation Centre
11 Osmeña St.
South Admiral Village
Bgy Merville
Pgue.
MM 1760
Tel: 63 2 824 9595
Fax: 63 2 823 3742

Singapore

Christian Meditation Centre
9 Mayfield Avenue
Singapore 438 023
Tel: 65 348 6790
Fax: 65 348 7302

Thailand

Christian Meditation Centre
51, 1 Sedsiri Road
Bangkok 10400
Tel: 66 2 271 3295
Fax: 66 2 271 2632
E-mail: sketudat@mozart.inet.co.th

United Kingdom

Christian Meditation Centre
The Hermitage
Monastery of Christ the King
29 Bramley Road
Cockfosters
London N14 4HE
Tel/Fax: 44 181 441 0680
E-mail: cmcuk@compuserve.com

United States

Christian Meditation Centre
193 Wilton Road West
Ridgefield, CT 06877
Tel: 1 203 438 2440
E-mail: pgulick@cwix.com

Christian Meditation on the Internet

Visit the World Community for Christian Meditation website at www.wccm.org